500 Days

The Explosive *True Story* of Medical Malpractice and One Woman's Fight to Live

Jo Ann Wills

Darby Press

Simpsonville, Kentucky

Copyright © 2022 by Jo Ann Wills

Darby Press
PO Box 768
Simpsonville, KY
www.DARBYPRESS.com

This book is a true story. The conversations and events are based on interrogatories, legal records, diaries, my personal notes, and memories. The names of the hospitals, doctors, and nurses have been changed.

500 Days: The Explosive True Story of Medical Malpractice and One Woman's Fight to Live
Author: Jo Ann Wills
Copyedit by Jaclyn Maria
ISBN Soft Cover 978-0-9992483-3-1
ISBN Electronic 978-0-9992483-4-8

A NOTE TO THE READER

On September 6, 2000, my mother underwent a surgical procedure to remove a stenosis or growth on her vocal cords that was obstructing her airway. The stenosis had begun several months earlier when Dr. Robinson, a pulmonologist, was called for a consult during my mother's visit to the ER of the Municipal Hospital.

Dr. Robinson became mother's pulmonologist and began treating her stenosis. The primary problem was the growth of scar tissue around the vocal cords that affects her ability to breath.

Over a period of months, Dr. Robinson would perform three laser procedures on my mother's throat. He also inserted a metal stent in an attempt to keep her airway open. None of this worked. In the end, he decided to use an oxygen-fed laser on her throat to "speed up" the process of removing the stenosis. This is where our trouble began.

We later discovered that he had no experience with the new oxygen-fed laser. He proceeded with reckless disregard for my mother's safety to perform a procedure using an instrument he was not qualified nor certified to use. As one might expect, things went wrong—terribly, irrevocably wrong.

He changed all of our lives that day. In seconds, we went from a "simple" procedure to a life-threatening nightmare that would last for 500 days.

As a child growing up in the 50s, our family was one unit. Dad worked while Mom took care of my two younger sisters and me. She was a stay-at-home mom with all the duties and responsibilities that entailed. Raised Catholic, the church was a regular part of our lives growing up. We were a happy family.

Over the years, Mom had her difficulties. She divorced and remarried, then became a widow. She also had health issues, but through it all she was always there for us—the heartbeat of our family.

When she had her first encounter with Dr. Robinson, Mom was seventy-four. In those days, (before Dr. Robinson) she was still independent and feeling well. Although she was legally blind, she loved to play cards, go out to dinner with her "girls" and spend time with friends.

On that day in September 2000, none of us knew the journey we had begun. Those 500 days have left their mark on our family.

On her deathbed my mother who could no longer talk, or even whisper, mouthed the words to me. "Tell my story," she said. "Tell them what happened to me."

I wrote this book to let others know that they can and should have a say in the medical care of their loved ones. Too often, we assume that the doctor is always right. Our part is only to observe their guidelines and obey their rules.

As modern consumers of medical treatment, we have a world of information readily available. We can and should question unfamiliar procedures or treatments. We should know that the doctor is certified and qualified on the equipment he is using or the medical device he is installing. This book is a cautionary tale of making assumptions when undergoing treatment.

After my experience, I now consider three things critical in monitoring and judging the medical care a loved one receives:

- Ask questions without guilt or feeling stupid.
- Do your research, if you need too, so you are comfortable asking informed questions.
- Never assume that the doctor is always right.

A Russian proverb says, "trust but verify". When it comes to medical treatment, this may be the best policy.

In this book, you will find helpful websites, books and organizations for patients, caregivers, and loved ones to help you navigate an increasingly complex and aloof medical establishment.

It is my sincere hope that in reading my mother's story you will learn about the simple courage of an ordinary woman and the strong ties that bind in families challenged by medical treatment gone wrong.

Jo Ann Wills

Mom, with this public revelation, I have fulfilled the promise I made to you . You are not for gotten.

"

...We also rejoice in our sufferings, because we know that suffering produces perseverance, perseverance, character, and character, hope. And hope does not disappoint us, because God has poured out his love into our hearts by the Holy Spirit whom he has given us.

— (NIV) Romans 5:3

PROLOGUE

In life, so many things begin with a conversation. For our family, it was a meeting during an examination in the emergency room of a local hospital. A simple, fateful meeting and ensuing conversation, no longer than three minutes, set in motion a tsunami of hardship and grief upon our family.

I have since come to realize that chance encounters, whether great or small, beneficial or detrimental, produce changes in our lives. As a tiny

rudder steers a mighty ship, so a chance conversation spun our lives out of control. Like a slow motion avalanche, it buried us all. Deep. Wet.
Suffocating.

CHAPTER ONE

Dr. Robinson

May 2000

It was a lovely spring day in May. Mildred Yager, my mother was retired from American Advertising, where she had worked for over eighteen years. Since leaving the company, she suffered with coronary heart disease and was diabetic, taking two insulin shots per day. Even though she was legally blind due to macular degeneration, she was independent. She had even taught herself how to cook her own meals using her peripheral vision.

My sisters and I were devoted to Mom. My younger sister, Wanda lived with Mom and Bill, Bill was Mom's second husband. Wanda chose never to marry, and when her job at Frito-Lay allowed her to buy her own home, Mom moved into Wanda's house. By that time, Bill had passed away from lung cancer, so it made sense that Mom and Wanda would live together.

Mom had been through so much medically, even breast cancer. Yet, she was active, enthusiastic and happy. All three of her daughters came to see her every week. We even took vacations together.

The last real vacation we took was to Hawaii. Mom couldn't walk long distances, but that didn't stop the fun. It was a wonderful trip. Shortly after that trip, Mom developed blurred vision. It was diagnosed as macular degeneration. I was so glad she had seen Hawaii before she lost her vision.

Mom prided herself on being as independent as possible. Being legally blind, she could no longer drive a car and relied on her daughters to get her back and forth to doctor appointments, the grocery store, and hair appointments. Living with

Wanda made those trips easier and because we were all so close, there were a lot of shopping trips, restaurant lunches and dinners, and visits to friends' houses.

She needed some help with her insulin shot because she couldn't see well enough to measure the dosage. Bravely, she gave herself all of her shots.

We were lucky because my youngest sister Janice was a cardiovascular technologist and worked at a local hospital for almost three decades. We relied on her expertise and familiarity with the doctors on call at the hospital when making medical decisions for Mom.

In early 2000, Mom's congestive heart failure was becoming more problematic. She was retaining fluid, experiencing shortness of breath and feeling tired. The winter months were hard, the cold weather taxing even healthy people. She hung in there through the cold but as spring approached, things worsened.

One afternoon, she was extra tired and having trouble breathing. Janice called me at work to discuss what to do. We both agreed it was time to take her to the emergency room.

Janice called the ambulance and they took Mom to the Municipal Hospital ER. Janice met the ambulance at the hospital. I meet them both as soon as I got off work.

By happenstance or fate, Mother's regular doctor was not on call that day. She saw a doctor she had not seen before, Dr. Aspen. Dr. Aspen was not as familiar with my mother's case, especially with her breathing issues. He wanted a pulmonary specialist to see her. He talked to Janice about bringing in a pulmonary specialist, Dr. Robinson.

Mom was struggling to breath during the ambulance ride to the hospital. The para-medic on duty intubated her through her nose to make her breathing easier. I think Dr. Aspen wanted to make sure that Mom's breathing issues could be resolved.

Janice knew of Dr. Robinson because he practiced at Municipal Hospital where she worked in the catheter lab. She told me that she had heard that he was an "aggressive" doctor. However, she trusted him because he was a staff doctor. She agreed to have Dr. Robinson 'take a look' at Mom.

They talked for the first time during that fateful E R visit.

When I arrived at the E R, a man clad in a doctor's smock with a white plastic ID tag hanging from his neck, bumped into me in the hallway. He stepped on my foot. Instead of apologizing to me, he said, "You are in my way." It struck me as the height of arrogance, but I had no idea who he was, nor did I care.

When I met Janice outside Mom's room, she looked down the hall past me. "Oh, Jo Ann, here comes Dr. Robinson, Mom's new doctor."

When I turned to greet him, the arrogant man had stepped on my foot, telling me that I was "in his way." I said hello and excused myself. I told Janice I was going for coffee.

When I returned the doctor was gone. I told Janice about my chance meeting with the good Dr. Robinson and our quick exchange in the hallway. "Janice," I said, "this guy is rude and arrogant." What's that old Bible verse? Pride goeth before the fall." I had to be honest with her. "Janice, this guy is not my choice for Mom's doctor. He's not friendly."

"Oh, Jo Ann, you are being silly. He has been around here for a while. He is a pulmonary specialist and Mom needs that expertise. With Mom's stenosis, we need a pulmonologist on her medical team. We should go with him."

Janice reminded me that if we eliminated doctors based on arrogance, we would eliminate most doctors in any hospital. We both laughed. I couldn't argue with her logic. I acquiesced.

Dr. Robinson walked into my mother's room to assess her condition. After seeing Mom, he felt that the nasal intubation was not working properly. He removed it and inserted a new tube into her throat.

When he had finished the procedure, he spoke to us in the hallway. "I had a lot of trouble intubating her lungs," he said. "I had to be very aggressive in getting the tube down her throat." There was that word again, "aggressive." I just wasn't getting any warm fuzzies from this guy. I thought to myself, *maybe they are right. I am not a medical person. I don't like this doctor, but even though I don't like him, maybe it will be okay.*

I deferred to Janice's medical expertise and her familiarity with hospital physicians. In hindsight, that was a mistake. Janice had no way of knowing what would happen, but I still remember that nagging feeling that something wasn't right with Dr. Robinson. I so wish that I had listened to that inner voice and insisted we get another physician.

In the future, I would give credence to that "gut" feeling or "small voice." I now believe that it is trying to guide us toward a better decision. We often ignore that voice. We do so at our peril.

Although Janice had no training as an RN, she was skilled at her job and was around doctors and nurses every working day. As a hospital employee, we had the comfort of knowing Janice could check on Mom every day. We did most if not all of Mom's medical procedures at Municipal Hospital.

When I look back on it, I see that our conversation with Dr. Robinson had set the pattern for increasingly problematic medical interventions.

Sometimes in the still of the night, I asked myself what might have been. What if I had paid more attention to my gut feeling?

***

Mildred Louise Todd Rusche Yager married twice. Even though she was a devotedCatholic, all of her life, her first marriage to our father, George Martin Rusche, ended in divorce.

I still remember our old house on 35th and Main Streets. I remember the October day that Mom and Dad drove up with our new baby sister, Janice Kay. I was going on five -years -old and Wanda was three. As the oldest, I am the memory keeper.

Mom was always an avid card player. As a "permanent redhead", she had the fire and spirit to match. She loved getting together with her ladies group each week. They took turns visiting one an-other's houses and playing cards.

When the three of us were little, o nce a week Mom would treat us to candies at the local grocery store. That was the highlight of t   he week. If we were poor, and we certainly were not well off in those days, we never realized it. My childhood was full of love and contentment. I had what I needed and wanted. The love of my sisters and my mom and dad.

Church was an anchor for our family   in those early days. We went every week and often in the middle of the week for extra-curricular activities.

One Saturday afternoon, Wanda and I had stopped at the corner grocery store. A kindly older man, Mr. Manning, owned the store. In the front of the store, there was a toy rack. I always headed straight for that rack when I came in with Mom. Mom wasn't with me this day so I spent a few minutes all alone watching over a toy bird. After some moments of doubt, I decided to go for it. I grabbed the bird, held it tightly in my hand and ran out the door like a mouse being chased by an owl. I ran with all my might, my accomplice, my little sister Wanda was in hot pursuit. I ran across the alley and into our back yard. Safe—or so I thought.

Once inside, I stashed the bird behind the couch—out of sight from prying eyes. There was only one problem. My little sister, only three years old, kept running behind the couch to sneak-a-peak at our newest stow-a-way.

All mothers seem to have "eyes in the back of their heads." My mother noticed Wanda's surreptitious behavior and asked me, as the oldest,

"What is going on behind the couch, Jo?" As she poses the question, she reaches down behind the couch to find my stash. Game over.

"Where did you get this toy, Jo Ann?" It was obviously a rhetorical question. A cool-hand-Luke, I was not. I burst into tears and made my full confession.

"I—. Took—. It—. From—. Mr. Manning's store."

My shame and humiliation complete, Mom replies. "Young lady, you take that toy back to Mr. Manning this instant. I want you to apologize to Mr. Manning for taking something that doesn't belong to you."

"Yes, Mama." Off I went to repent of my sins. Mr. Manning, God rest his soul, was quick to forgive and to forget.

***

After the emergency room visit and Mom's encounter with Dr. Robinson, her stenosis became progressively worse. Stenosis happens when the breathing channel begins to close. Although caused by a variety of medical conditions, the buildup of scar tissue blocking the airway is often the problem. Scar tissue was the culprit in Mom's case A problem that worsened after Dr. Robinson's first "aggressive" treatment in the ER. From that moment on, Mom needed frequent intervention to remove the growing scar tissue.

To this day, I believe that Dr. Robinson's intubation lead to a more rapid buildup of scar tissue in her airway.

CHAPTER TWO

The Early Years

My mom was a yodeler. Yes. She could yodel. I'm not sure where or how she acquired the skill. It's something of a lost art. The last time I saw someone yodel was in the original version of the Shirley Temple movie, *Heidi.*

When I was six our family moved to a small house at 127 North 37 th Street. It was a typical depression era house with a large partially enclosed front porch and two upstairs attic bedrooms. Mom would often come upstairs at night to tuck us in and would treat us to a yodeling session.

The sound fascinated me but I could never duplicate it. She had a wonderful singing voice. I didn't realize it then, but to be able to yodel you need a lot of voice control and good breathing.

Mother loved to sing around the house. I can still hear her singing the 1941 hit "Boogie Woogie Bugle Boy of Company B." The original recording was by the Andrews Sisters, but became popular again in 1971 when Bette Midler recorded it. She also loved to sing tunes by Bing Crosby, Dean Martin, and Patsy Cline.

In our house if the 45 record wasn't spinning on the "hi-fi" then the small hand organ was playing. My mother's hands racing across the keys as she sang church hymns. It is ironic to think of those times now and remember her in the hospital bed unable to speak.

Our front porch was the "go-to" porch for all the neighborhood kids. They would all come over and hangout. Mom loved it because she always said, "When the kids are on our porch, I don't have to worry about where my girls are or what they are doing."

My dad was a guard at the local skating rink. He first met Mom when she used to skate there. He always told us he fell in love with her red hair. Mom maintained that red hair until the day she died. I can't imagine my mother with any other hair color.

***

Over the next three months, Mother's condition would worsen. The trips to the ER for shortness of breath became more frequent. Through each of these episodes, Dr. Robinson treated her either directly or through phone consolation during her ER visits.

Through it all, Mom was always her old self. She was slower, but still eager to have a meal in a restaurant, have some hardy laughs with her pals in her card club, or enjoy a night out at the movies with her daughters.

CHAPTER THREE

The Fire

In June, Mother's breathing difficulties continued. Dr. Robinson was treating her for tracheal stenosis. My mother was terrified of losing her voice. She would often tell us before a treatment, "Don't let them take my voice. I don't want to come out of here without my voice."

As the weeks and months passed, Dr. Robinson did three separate treatments. The first treatment he tried to cut out scar tissue using a scalpel. He couldn't remove much scar tissue. It grew back quickly.

The second treatment, he decided to use the YAG Laser. Each time, relief was short-lived. The stenosis would return and so would Mom's breathing troubles.

Dr. Robinson wanted to put in a stent during the first treatment but Janice was against it. By the time Mom needed a third treatment, Dr. Robinson had talked Janice into allowing him to insert a metal stent.

Following that procedure, she was able to leave the hospital in a couple of days. She was better for a time, but six weeks after her third laser treatment and the installation of the stent, her breathing again became labored.

Janice called Dr. Robinson and told him Mom was having trouble breathing again. He said to 'bring her in'. He thought she would need a fourth laser treatment.

They took Mom to the laser procedural room. He told Janice that the stent needed to come out because it wasn't the right size. The scar tissue had already grown over the stent, covering it up. The stent, made of steel, had a basket weave pattern. The scar tissue had grown through and then over the holes in the stent. This was a bad situation. A lot of tissue had to be cut away to remove the stent. Not only scar tissue but native tissue as well. The date was September 5, 2000. The day before the FIRE.

The procedure, as my sisters and I understood it, was to remove some of the scar tissue, then to use a laser to remove the remaining tissue and the stent.

September 5, 2000—Day before the Fire

That morning they took Mom to the operating room. We said our goodbyes and I told her it would all be fine and that Janice, Wanda, and I would be there when she woke up. Mom seemed fine and ready to remove the stent and scar tissue the next morning when the doctor would use the laser to finish the procedure.

September 6, 2000—Day of the Fire

The last thing she said to me was, "Jo Ann, don't let me come out with one of those voice box-es. I don't want to lose my voice."

I told her that would never happen, they were just going to remove the stent and everything would be fine. That conversation still haunts me.

We said our goodbyes before they took he r to the operating room. I never spoke to Dr. Robinson before the procedure.

The morning of September 6, only Janice and I were in the waiting room. Wanda was working that day. I recall speaking briefly to the anesthesiologist that morning. Those conversations are usually brief and routine. More about reassuring the loved ones than they are about the procedure itself.

It seemed like we sat in the waiting room for hours with no word from the doctors. I am sure it wasn't that long, but it seemed like a long time. I told Janice I needed a cup of coffee. "I've got to have a cup of coffee, Janice," I told her. "I'll be right back. I won't be gone long."

When I walked back into the waiting room, coffee still in hand. Something was wrong. Janice was sitting with Dr. Robinson and she was sobbing. Great racks of grief poured out of her. Janice was not one to cry. *This can't be good,* I thought.

"Janice … Janice, what's wrong?" I sat down in a chair next to her and across from the doctor.

"It's bad, Jo Ann. It's bad," she said. Then she dropped her head to her hands and began sobbing again.

"What's bad, Janice? Tell me ... what is bad? Has something happened to Mom?" I could feel the high pitch of my voice. I knew I was almost shouting, but I was helpless to stop it.

"There was a fire," she fumbled the words. It came out like a question. I think she was trying to wrap her head around it.

"A fire? What do you mean? A fire—where?" I asked. "Oh my God, Janice, what are you telling me? Is she—is Mom ... okay?" I was in full-blown panic. "Is she alive?" Nearly hysterical, I looked at Dr. Robinson, my eyes pleading for an answer. He was stoic. Offered no information, no explanation, and no comfort.

"DID YOU SET MY MOTHER ON FIRE?" I was shouting and powerless to stop.

He held his head in his hands, refusing to look up. His head shook slightly. He shrugged his shoulders as if to say, "Yes, I guess I did."

"Is my mother even ALIVE?" I was trembling. He shook his head, "Yes, she is still alive," he whispered.

"What state is she in? " I look around the waiting room, hoping for someone in authority who can explain this nightmare to me. I say aloud to no one and to everyone in the room, "Will somebody please tell me what's happened to my mother?"

I looked at Janice. "We've got to get it together, Jo," she said. "We've just got to get it together. We've got to get the facts together and find out what exactly happened in there."

"I want to know what happened," I demanded. The doctor looked at me. "Did you set my mother on fire? If you set my mother on fire I'll ..," My hand balled into a fist. Dr. Robinson interrupted me.

He shrugged his shoulders and folded his arms across his chest. "I'm not sure what happened ... I don't know."

"You—don't—know—. You don't know what happened to my mother." Seconds later a nurse was standing beside me. She was dressed in operating room garb. I looked into her eyes. "You saw my mother on fire? Did you see my mother on fire?"

Another doctor had joined us. I think it was Dr. Raka; a doctor I thought was the anesthesiologist. I had spoken to him earlier that morning.

Dr. Raka answered, "Yes, I saw your mother on fire. It was frightening. The flames were shooting out of her mouth. I had to put out the fire inside her mouth. I yanked the burning laser out of her throat. It was still burning. The laser was still on fire. I threw it across the room. It continued to burn. Someone put it out."

A shock wave rippled through my body. I could feel the hairs on my neck stand on end. I was terrified. As if from a dream I heard Dr. Robinson say to Janice, "You know, Janice, freaky things happen. You never really know why they happen but they do. We don't know ... what causes these things. Freaky things can happen with lasers."

Janice seemed encased in a calming fog. Through that fog she said, "No, Dr. Robinson—no—. I don't know about 'freaky things' with lasers. Freaky things don't happen in the Cath lab. We work with lasers there too, but we don't set people on fire."

"I want to know what happened in there," I demanded. "What state is she in? What state is my mother in?

Janice looks at me and repeated, "We've just got to get it together, we got to get the facts together … we have to find out what happened. We don't know anything."

It was too much. Medical professionals surrounded me. They had all been in the room when the Fire happened. No one was saying anything.

It was then that a nurse we knew, a friend of Janice's, thrust a consent form into our hands. It was consent to do a trach. "Here," she held the paper out to me, "you need to sign this form so we can get this tracheostomy in. She needs this. She needs it right now. It was a nightmare." The nurse's hand was trembling. Whatever had happened in that OR had shaken her to the core.

Janice signed the form. After she left, Janice's hospital supervisor asked how we were holding up. "I heard something terrible happened this morning Janice, are you okay? Is your Mom okay?"

She had no idea what had happened to Mom but word about the "incident" had already hit the hospital's coconut express.

As we sat there, Dr. Raka came running into the waiting room. His face was shiny from sweat. He was visibly upset—shaken.

"She is stable right now," he told me. "They are doing the tracheostomy." Dr. Raka was the attending physician, not the anesthesiologist. The good news was he had reacted quickly and pulled the laser out of mother's throat and put out the fire. He had saved her life. I was grateful.

Janice and I were escorted to a private waiting room where we could deal with our emotions privately. The hospital didn't want their dirty laundry aired in a public waiting room. We waited all afternoon without learning any more details on my mother's condition.

Around four o'clock that afternoon, a nurse came to give us an update. She spoke to Janice first. "It was awful Janice. We had to give our staff counseling. The trauma was too much for some of them. They've never experienced anything like that before."

Janice was incredulous. "You mean to tell me that the nurses and doctors have all received counseling and we have been sitting here with no one to even advise us of my mother's condition?"

"Well, Janice," she replied. "We have to take care of our employees. I know it seems out of order, but our employees are traumatized. Surely, you understand that we had to take care of them. One nurse had to go home she was so upset. The good news is your mother is stable."

Janice shook her head. "Good news? We have been waiting here all afternoon with no news ... good or bad. My mother and my sisters and I have been brutalized today. Do you understand that?" She had no answer. What could she say? This was wrong. It was just wrong.

A few minutes later, we were able to see Mom in the recovery room. She was in and out of unconsciousness. Unaware of what had happened to her. She did not find out what had happened for a few days. Two days later, one of the nurses told us that one of her doctors had explained to Mom what happened to her in the OR. During that explanation, Mom was alone with no family present. I think that was by design.

The tracheostomy is an incision in the throat to allow the patient to breathe through a tube inserted into the incision. Patients with permanent traches cannot speak. In my mother's case, the doctors would later tell us that her voice box was burned beyond repair. Removing the necrotic tissue had likely cost my mother her voice. She never spoke again.

My precious mother, who loved to sing and could yodel, would never speak or sing again.

CHAPTER FOUR

Dealing with a New Reality

Seeing Mom lying in recovery took me back to a trip we made with Mom when her stepmother, Lillian Todd ('Mamma Todd') was critically ill. Alice Litsey, my biological grandmother and Mom's birth mother, left Pawpaw Todd, along with her two children (my mother and her sister, my Aunt Ethel) when Mom was three-years-old and Aunt Ethel was six. Alice's abandonment devastated my mother and Ethel. The oral history of the family says that Alice ran off with another man.

Nearly two years after Alice left him,   Papaw Todd remarried a younger woman, Lilian Young. Lillian was a child herself, only fifteen years old when she and my grandfather were married. Despite the difference in age, and Lillian's youth, she was a wonderful wife and stepmother.

Together Lillian and Pawpaw Todd created a stable home life for my Mom and Aunt Ethel. They were only three and six years old when Lillian became their stepmother.

My mother would not see or hear from her birth mother for the next twenty years. Lillian was a loving stepmother and had sustained Mom through those tough years after being abandoned. According to Mom, her wayward and missing mother did come back to town when she needed money and a place to stay. Both Mom and Aunt Ethel were in their twenties when their biological mother came back home.

Alice didn't hesitate to ask her two abandoned daughters for help. To their credit, neither my Mother nor Aunt Ethel turned their backs on her.

They helped in any way they could. Both felt it was their moral and Christian duty.

The last time Alice reconnected with her children was after she remarried for the last time. Her new husband's name was Roy O'Leary. He was a wonderful man and loved kids. Well-to-do, he lavished us with gifts, trips and special treats. Alice was along for the ride, but put a good face on being close to her daughters and grandchildren. When Roy O'Leary passed away from a heart attack a few years later, we were devastated.

Alice inherited Roy's money and ran off with some new "friends". She didn't come back again until the money was gone and she needed a place to stay to live out her elderly years. By the time she came back, her oldest daughter, my Aunt Ethel had passed away from colon cancer. Alice didn't know her daughter had passed. When she found out all she said was, "that's too bad." Aunt Ethel was only forty-eight years old when she passed.

I share this story because as I look back on my mom's and Aunt Ethel's lives, I see a correlation between that early abandonment and suffering many physical ailments as grown women. I sometimes wonder if childhood hurts that run deep can fester in the body over time and in ways we don't understand, eventually cause us to become sick.

When Pawpaw Todd passed away, Lillian soon remarried and moved with her new husband to Pittsburgh. In 1994, Mamma Lillian was hospitalized—her condition grave.

We got a call from my Aunt Patty. "Lillian is very sick," she told us. "She is in a hospital in Pittsburgh. I think if you can, you girls should take your mother to see her. They were always so close."

Mother's health was not the best. She was sixty-two and suffering from diabetes, macular degeneration, and other ailments. Still, she wanted desperately to make the trip and we wanted to help her if we could.

We took Mom to see her stepmother one last time. It was a 400-mile bus ride and the trip was hard on everyone, especially Mom. When we finally got to the hospital to see Lillian,   I watched as Mom sat beside her bed and tenderly held her hand. The love in their eyes was wonderful and heartbreaking.

Her eyes filled with tears, Mom thanked Lillian for all she had done for her as a child. As Mom put it, "you gave me back my life, Lillian. How can I ever repay you for that?" It was a cherished moment and a testament to how one person can affect in a positive way the lives of children. Because Lillian found it in her heart to love two little girls who needed a mother's touch, my mother was able to become the loving parent that she was to us.

Lillian passed away peacefully in her sleep several weeks later. To this day, I am so thankful that we made the commitment to Mom to take her to see her beautiful stepmother.

Seeing Mom lying so quietly in bed somehow took me back to that day. How would I ever make this medical nightmare right for my mother?

There was no way I could. There is no way anyone could. It was a most trying day.

When Janice signed the consent form for Dr. Robinson to use the laser, I believe she had serious reservations because it used oxygen. Anytime there is oxygen and a laser, there is a chance of fire if used improperly. The doctor assured Janice that he was comfortable with the new laser. He had used the YAG laser two times before on mother's throat without mishap.

Dr. Robinson had been downright cocky about his "skill" and "knowledge" of this equipment. As it turned out, he had neither skill nor knowledge with the new laser.

CHAPTER FIVE

The First Several Days

It is eight hours after Mom's throat, vocal cords, and lungs were burned. We don't know the extent of the damage but we are beginning to guess that it is extensive.

Mother rests in her bed, coming in and out of sleep. She is comfortable; the pain medication administered before and after the procedure is still doing its job.

Dr. Robinson comes into her room. He is smiling. I am appalled at his lack of empathy. "She seems to be doing pretty well, considering what she's been through." His smile belies the grave situation in which we find ourselves.

My sister's and I say nothing. We just look at him as though he has two heads ... perhaps he does.

None of the hospital administrators had bothered to speak to us or to see how Mom was doing. We had no real information on what happened and why. To say it was a difficult time is an understatement.

For Mom, this is a catastrophic medical hardship in a lifetime of such hardships. This was not her fault; it was negligence, and in my opinion greed on the part of Dr. Robinson. He wanted to use that particular laser because it would save him time.

Mother has a trach and is on a ventilator. She appears to be resting comfortably—as comfortably as one can on a ventilator in the intensive care unit.

The next morning, Dr. Robinson pays another visit. "I wanted you to know that I didn't sleep last night. I'm very upset with what happened in the operating room, but your mom is doing well. She has a little pulmonary edema (fluid on the lungs) but she is doing okay. I would like to do a bronchoscopy on Saturday. I want to see how badly she is burned."

Janice looked at Dr. Robinson and said, "This is a fucking nightmare ...a fucking nightmare."

"I know," he said. I wondered if he had any idea what we were going through. Any idea at all.

Day Three: September 9, 2000

By day three, the post-surgical medication is wearing off, and Mom is more aware of her situation, and of the pain and discomfort. She has tears in her eyes. I think she is trying to process the bad dream that has become her reality.

A few days pass and Mom seemed to be doing better. Two days later, I walk into her room after work and find her sitting up in a chair. I could tell by the twinkle in Mom's eye that she was proud of herself and happy to be out of bed.

Later that afternoon, the nurse on duty came into the room. She told us that Dr. Raka, the attending thoracic surgeon during Mom's Fire had explained to Mom that her throat and lungs had been burned. I would later learn that all of the laser procedures require a n attending surgeon be present in case of an accident, or in our case, a catastrophe.

"Dr. Raka told Mom everything about the FIRE," the nurse said.

"Everything?" I asked. "How did she take it?"

"He said she took it 'very well.'" The nurse took Mom's blood pressure then left the room. I wasn't sure if that was true or not. Why was Mom told about the surgery and the FIRE while she was alone—without her family? Why had Mom been given an account of what happened while we still had no real knowledge of what happened in that operating room?

One of the problems with not being able to speak is you cannot advocate for yourself. Since Mom was also legally blind, she couldn't write anything. Janice, having worked in the hospital for twenty-nine years understood this predicament better than Wanda or me.

She decided to take a leave of absence from the hospital so she could act as Mom's medical advocate. It was a wise decision. It was a critical time for Mom and no one knew how long she would be hospitalized.

Mom does a lot of coughing, which most trach patients do. It comes with the territory. With a trach, you are always minutes away from suffocating on your own fluids. Sadly, without it she cannot breathe at all.

Mom has a feeding tube and Dr. Robinson told us she cannot eat regular food. We would find out later that she could eat. Dr. Robinson also told us "her lungs are not burned." We would later find out her lungs were burned.

Nothing Dr. Robinson told us was true. He had through haste and negligence, burned my mother's insides in a most barbaric way. He was consistently in denial until the day we fired him as mother's physician.

CHAPTER SIX

The First 30 Days

As the days turned into weeks, Mom had her good days and bad. So did my sisters and me. Her vocal cords were damaged beyond repair. Mom could only mouth words. Sometimes, in the early days, she could manage a hoarse whisper but once the scar tissue began to grow, she lost her voice for good.

Her body was constantly trying to slough off the necrotic tissue from her throat and lungs. Since she was using a trach, her airway needed frequent clearing. This is accomplished by doing a bronchoscopy. A bronchoscopy lasts at least 30 minutes, but can last up to four hours including prep and recovery time.

To get Mom ready for the procedure, the nurses would administer a mild sedative by injecting it into her intravenous (IV) line. Liquid medicine, sprayed into the nose, helps numb the area and retard the gag reflex.

The procedure is painful and frightening. A long thin tube is pushed down the throat. It has a camera so that the clinician can see the patient's airway. Once the tube is all the way in, and pictures are taken, the tube is pulled out the way it came. This helps clear the airway of mucus and wash away the sloughed off necrotic tissue. Mom would have over 40 of these procedures during her hospital stay.

On the "bronch-days", we stayed with her all day. They were rough on everyone. On the first bronch, Mom's throat was too swollen to "see" the vocal cords. She developed pneumonia with a low-grade fever.

September 15, 2000

We have regained some of our emotional footing and are thinking with clearer heads.

Early that morning, two doctors from the hospital drop by to check on Mom. Dr. Kara and Dr.

Timothy. Dr. Timothy looked at us and asked, "Are you two still planning to have Dr. Robinson care for your mother?"

Janice answers, "Are you willing to take over her care?"

"Of course we will," said Dr. Timothy.

"Gladly," said Dr. Kara.

"Good," Janice replied, "it's decided then." A sense of relief was written all over her face. "It looks like we have two new doctors, Jo Ann."

"You know, Janice," Dr. Timothy told her, "Dr. Robinson had never done a procedure like he did on your mother using that particular laser ... not ever. Dr. Robinson wasn't certified to use that laser at Municipal Hospital."

Later that day, Dr. Robinson came to see Mom. "How is the patient today?" he asked. He smiles as if nothing bad has happened. Just a "little mishap in the OR." Janice said nothing, at first. When he goes toward Mom's bed, we both freeze. Janice speaks, "Dr. Robinson, your services are no longer needed here."

"Nor wanted," I added. Looking stunned, he turns and leaves the room. Perhaps he is thinking what we are; that mother's condition is not the re-sult of a "mishap' but of hard, cold negligence.

For the first time since September 6, the doc-tors tell us we don't have to stay the night. "Your mom is in good hands," they tell us.

Journal Entries:
September 16, 2000

When I get to the hospital this morning, Mom is sitting up in a ch air. I am elated. She has a little color in her face and her eyes twinkle. I discover later that the color is because her white blood count is elevated, it has doubled from the day before. She has a lung in-fection.

September 17, 2000

The doctors think Mom is de-pressed.I cannot blame her for that. He suggests a mild anti-depressant. At this point, we are relying on her new doc-tors to tell us what is best. I am not sure I ever want to rely on a ny doctor again.

The truth is I am overwhelmed. My sisters and I agree to the anti-depressants.

At night, when Janice, Wanda and I get ready to leave the hospital Mom cries. Her beautiful eyes well up with tears. I hope the anti-depressants begin to do their magic soon.

We still haven't heard from anyone in hospital administration about what happened in the OR. I can't imagine why someone hasn't contacted us. No doubt, their attorneys have advised them not to speak with us.

September 21, 2000

We finally hear from the hospital administration. Mel Updraft, a hospital attorney tells us that Emergency Care Research Institute, an independent non-profit that researches the best approaches to improving patient care will be investigating the "incident." Ms. Updraft thinks the investigation will take six months.

Janice and I have a long discussion about legal protection for our family and for Mom. We decide to contact an attorney.

Three weeks after the Fire, we hire Minor and Munich to represent us.

I realize that each day, morning-to-lunch, lunch-to-dinner, even hour-to-hour, mother's condition fluctuates from good, to not so good, too bad—a daily roller coaster ride.

I keep thinking of the old "Star Trek" series on TV. I can hear Captain Kirk yelling to "Scotty" the Scottish engineer in charge of Enterprises mechanicals, "Beam me up, Scotty. Beam me up!"

Finally, on September 30 we get to move Mom out of intensive care and into the ventilator care unit (VCR).

CHAPTER SEVEN

October: 60 Days

My mother has a PICC line in her arm. The nurses use it to administer drugs and IVs so they will not have to stick her continually. It is a small compensation, but we will take all that we can get.

Mom takes pain meds on most days. She seems very tired. Her body is exhausted from fighting off constant infections while trying to repair the damage to her throat, vocal cords and lungs.

She still needs to be suctioned on a regular basis and every four hours she has a breathing treatment. No wonder she is tired. We are all tired.

Sometimes when I visit, I don't say much. We just smile at each other. She is happy that we are together. Even as the exhaustion creeps up on me, I am happy to be there. It is the least I can do. Look at what she did for us.

I can't help wondering what she is thinking. Why does she fight so hard? I sit beside her, contemplating what has happened to her when she raises her hand to get my attention.

I look up. She is trying to tell me something. "What is it, Mom? What do you want to tell me?"

She mouths the words slowly, so I will understand. "Tell them," she says.

"Tell them? Mom, are you saying 'tell them?'"

She nods her head 'yes'. She mouths more words. "My story ...tell ...them ...my ...story."

Finally, I get it. "You want me to tell them your story. I understand." I did understand. Mom wanted me to write her story. As a kid, I used to makeup stories for her. Sometimes I would write them down, sometimes not. She loved it. Maybe she knew that writing this book was both our destinies.

That conversation changed me. From that day forward, I was determined, no matter the outcome, to fulfill her wish.

Journal Entries:

October 5, 2000

It is not a good day. Mom got up to walk today and when she sat down, she vomited all over the place. I called the nurse and they turned off her feeding tube. They x-ray her stomach, no problems there, but she is sick the rest of the day.

They give her something f or nausea but it doesn't help. She is coughing and vomiting most of the day. This is a bad day.

October 8, 2000.

When the doctor comes in today, I tell him, " I think it's time to cut back on the Zoloft meds. All she does is sleep. That can't be good for her." He agrees to cut it back.

October 17, 2000

T hings seem to be improving but I know better than to count on the improvements I see …just yet. E xperience has taught me how quickly her condition can deteriorate. Still, I revel in the small victories she experiences when they happen.

The last couple of days she has been taking wheel-chair rides up and down the hallway. Just getting out of her room seems to warm her spirits. We fix her hair today. She gets the works, makeup, hair combed and styled, even her finger and toenails boast a bright red. We have a good time and she manages to smile and even come close to laughing a few times.

As a caregiver, I have learned to relish these moments of fun and light-heartedness. There is always time to be sad and depressed. When these fun moments happen, we take full advantage of them.

She is still on a feeding tube and the doctor wants to do another bronch tomorrow or the next day. I hat e those days. It seems like every time she is feeling stronger, there is another pro-cedure that takes the wind out of her.

October 19, 2000

Dr. Kara is in the room early to check on Mom before her bronch. He comes to see us after the procedure and tells us that she is getting scaring on her right lung. This is not good news. He tells us she may never be able to eat or drink again normally. Knowin g she may have to live like this the rest of her life isn't the scariest thing he tells us that morning. He also tells us he doesn't know how to treat her. He has never seen anything like this before and so he is trying things that he thinks will help her, but no one can be sure.

He even admits to us that he is looking on the Internet in hopes of

finding another doctor who has experience with something like this and has
workable methods to treat it.

We appreciate his candor and are
more worried now than ever. Lord,
please help us find someone who can
help.

October 27, 2000

Mom has another b ronch and two
more scheduled for this week. These
are tough days. I go home feeling hol-
lowed out and exhausted. I lay down to
sleep and start to cry. After an   hour,
the tears dry up and I am able to fall
asleep. We need help. This is overtak-
ing our family.

October 30, 2000

Dr. Timothy calls to tell me that he
may have found a specialist to help us.
The doctor he found practices at Bos-

ton General. He may have two other doctors lined up for us as well.

During this conversation, Dr. Timothy asked me, "Jo Ann, are you okay? Are you feeling all right? You seem a little tired and distracted."

"Yes," I answer, "I'm fine."

"No, you are not fine," he replies. "You know, Jo Ann, it doesn't do your Mom any good for you to wear yourself out. You have to take care of yourself. Caregiving is not a sprint—it is a marathon. You have to make sure you have rest and time away. A day away from the hospital will do wonders."

I know on some level that what he tells me is true, but I can't seem to stop doing what I'm doing. If I don't go to the hospital one day, I feel guilty. The truth is, to be the most effective patient advocate you can be, you need to take some time off. A two-hour walk in the sunshine while your charge is sleeping or resting can put a new spring in your step.

October 31, 2000

Mom seems to be having a good day today. She is alert and feeling better. Please, Lord, let her get stronger. Help us to overcome this.

CHAPTER EIGHT

November: 90 Days

It's November 8 and Mom has a bronch today. She sleeps for several hours. I know the next day or two will be tough days for her.

Dr. Timothy made his rounds this morning. He told us the scar tissue is building in her airways and into the lungs. We are devastated. All of us are exhausted and having a difficult time coping. Some days it seems that if it were not for bad news, we would have no news at all.

Dr. Kara wants to consult with a thoracic surgeon. We are fine with that but anxious to see steady improvement and some rest from the relentless onslaught of bad news.

Mom has gone several days being able to eat soft foods like cream of wheat, but now, according to her doctors, she will have to go back on a feeding tube. That process is painful. Mom cries when the nurse inserts the feeding tube.

We all cry together. It does not help the pain but somehow it helps us to keep moving forward. I feel sorry for her doctors. They have not seen this type of injury before. They don't know how to treat it. They do stopgap measures to keep her airway open, but overall, they are losing ground.

Journal Entries:

November 10, 2000

Even though Mom seems depressed over the feeding tube, she is a real trooper. The nurses love her and she is a big hit in V C U. I hope it stays that way.

November 17, 2000

Janice decides to do Mom's hair and nails. It   never fails to   cheer her up. Thank go odness for root touchup dye. It is tough doing Mom's roots in a hos-pital bed, but Janice insists that she look good. She believes it makes her feel better about everything. I have to say I agree with her.

November 21, 2000

Dr. Timothy dilates   the main air-way and injects steroids again. He de-cides against a stent or laser treatment for now. The good doctor tells us that Mom will have a trach for life. We hope against hope that he is wrong. He also tells us she has a small nod ule on her lung. "It's most likely scar tissue," he tells us.

November 23, 2000

It is Thanksgiving Day. We have a huge chipboard turkey mounted on the bulletin board in Mom's hospital room. There are turkey cards and lots of fall colored flowers but no m ention of food. Being on a feeding tube, we don't want to make a big deal about food.

I think back to my childhood memories of Thanksgiving. Mom always made us a hearty breakfast, early on Thanksgiving morning. Then we would get dressed and go to see our Aunts and Uncles and eat our way through the family gatherings. Thanksgiving was always   about family, hearth, and homestead for us.It still is today.

The whole family comes to see Mom. The grandchildren and spousesgather in her room . It is still all about family and being together.

November 29, 2000

The feeding tube is still in place. She complains of a stomachache. Another bronch today, which means at least two days of pain and feeling poorly.

The doctor decides to give her more steroids. A rough day.

December: 121 Days

It's December and the holidays are upon us. This will be the first time Mom has spent Christmas in the hospital. I am determined, as is Janice, to make this a wonderful Christmas holiday for her.

Journal Entry:
December 12, 2000

Mom's IV needed replacing. They took it out for a few days and then put in a new PICC line. Today the IV is returning blood. *Oh, God, please let all of this stop. We need your help.*

Janice spoke to Mark today, he and his partner are the investigators hired by the hospital to look into Mom's case. Mark gives Janice the number of one of the producers of the television show 20/20. He thinks we should contact them and go public with Mom's story. Both Janice and I feel that going public will just add another layer of complication to what we are already having a tough time dealing with. I put the number in my purse and never think about it again.

Mark tells us that the laser Dr. Robinson used for the procedure that burned Mom has checked out okay.

Finally, after months of waiting we know the truth. The laser was good. The Fire that changed all of our lives was never "equipment malfunction" or a "freaky thing that sometimes happens with lasers." The Fire was due to human error, not equipment malfunction.

All month we have been bringing in Christmas cards and hanging them in Mom's room. She has a four-foot Christmas tree, complete with lights sitting on her chest of drawers. We have strung lights around the window so that her room has a soft glow at night.

Some of the kids at my school where I work as a special education assistant have made greeting cards for mom. I love it. We tack the cards to the corkboard in her room.

Looking at the lights makes me think of those wonderful Christmas mornings as a child.

***

Mom and Dad would always put our presents under the tree after we went to bed on Christmas Eve. In our old house on 37th street, the living room was separated from the hall and stairway landing by a huge arched opening.

On Christmas Eve, Mom and Dad would hang a sheet across the archway. That meant that beyond the sheet was no-man's-land for my sisters and me. On the night before Christmas, Mom would feed us early and put us to bed. We would all give furtive glances at the sheet as we turned to climb the stairs to our   second-floor bedrooms. No one dared look beyond the sheet or venture a peek.

On Christmas morning, Mom would call from the bottom of the stairs, "Jo … Janice … Wanda … its Christmas morning. Time to get up and get ready for church."

Exited and jumping for joy, we would all clamor down the stairs. The sheet still blocking our view, we hurried into the kitchen to eat a hot breakfast. After breakfast, back up the stairs, and then dress for church. When we left for church, we had to exit through the back door. (The front door was in the living room, behind the sheet.)

Home from church, we entered once again through the back door where we all assembled at the landing at the foot of the stairs. Our backs to the sheet, we giggled in anticipation as we heard Dad rustle the sheet to pull it down and reveal our gifts, wrapped in colorful papers, and tucked neatly under the tree in three distinct piles labeled 'Janice', 'Jo', and 'Wanda.'

As we jumped and fidgeted, Dad would give the word, "Okay Mom, the girls can turn around now," he would tell mother.

Like three baby chicks turned loose for the first time in a new yard, we ran through the arch and into the living room. We ripped off the paper with great abandon, shards of glittery and colorful wrapping flew everywhere. Mom and Dad wore smiles a mile wide. I think they had more fun than we did.

This Christmas was not like those, but the memory of those Christmases long ago, still warmed our hearts today. Despite the circumstances, it was a good Christmas. Mom was feeling good and we were so glad to have her with us.

Journal Entry:

December 28, 2000

Dr. Kara does more blood gases today. The results are not good and he decides to put Mom back on a ventilator. This is a blow to all of us.

She can't talk but mouths to me, "Jo, am I okay? Am I okay?" she repeats.

"Yes, Mom. You are doing fine. You are just fine," I tell her hoping that the questions in my own mind don't show on my face. Relieved by my answer she drifts off to sleep.

An hour later she is awake feeling anxious and in pain. Dr. Kara orders morphine. She goes back to sleep but the look on her face tells me she is worried.

CHAPTER TEN

Jan-Feb: 180 Days

January and February were roller coaster months for all of us. Mom's health fluctuated from bad to better, than back again. We do our best to keep her spirits up. Her efforts to stay upbeat are obvious and appreciated. Every day I wonder how she endures it. The constant suctions, bronchs, blood tests, and endless hours in bed. The nurses clear her airways every two hours. Without it, she would suffocate. The suctioning goes on all night and all day. Getting uninterrupted sleep is impossible.

Journal Entries:

January 1, 2001

It is New Year's Day and my birthday—a good day. Her eyes are bright, she is awake and off the ventilator. She is able to sit in her chair and even walk a little. We spend the day together. Our habit over the years is to make a cake for everyone's birthdays. This year, we pass on the cake. It is just too hard to have cake knowing that Mom can't eat anything, much less cake.

We spent a wonderful day together. All of us grateful for   the blessings of a great day as a family.

January 31, 2001

Mom fails the swallowing test again, which means she will stay on the feeding tube. She is disappointed but Dr. Kara says her lungs are improving. She has a nagging infection in her right eye.

February 3, 2001

Dr. Kara does bronch number 24. She is tire d for two days. He also takes away her ice chips until Dr. Timothy comes back into town   on the twelfth. Mom is hopping mad. When you cannot eat, sucking on a few ice chips is a big deal. Mother is irate that she can no longer enjoy her ice snack. In a worl d where luxuries are   non-existent and pleasures can be   numbered on one hand, ice chips   become the moral equivalent of a juicy steak with a side of Caesar salad and a baked potato.

I will be glad when Dr. Timothy gets back in town and restores Mom's ice chip privileges.

February 13, 2001

Today Dr. Timothy performed   an-other bronch. Number 25. Mom is up-set. I see her tears and feel my own eyes begin to burn. How much more can she take? Every day I wonder how much more she can tolerate. We need some good news,*Lord. Please help us here.*

February 22, 2001

Today she developed vaginal bleeding. This is a first and no one seems to know why this is happening.

Dr. Timothy and Dr. Kara continue to look for a qualified physician to help direct Mom's treatment. I   cannot believe that in this vast country there is not one doctor who knows how to treat this type of wound.

Mom is able to sit in a chair for most of the day. She stares into the dist ance, lost in her own thoughts .

Sadly, we don't know what is on her mind because she can't talk. I think the depression is seeping into her bones and she is closing herself off. That scares me more than the constant onslaught of medical procedures and the complications of her healing.

In late February, we get great news. Dr. Timothy has located two more doctors, one in Cleveland and another in San Diego. That makes three doctors who might be able to help guide Mom's treatment plan.

Are they willing to take on her case? We are hopeful. After months of floundering around, not knowing how best to treat mom's injuries, a solution is in sight.

The doctor who seems most optimistic that he can help is in San Diego. It is a long way to go for treatment, but at this stage, we are willing to try anything. His name is Dr. Harley and he is the director of pulmonary diagnostics and an expert in the YAG lasers.

Dr. Harley has also invented his own stent for patients who need to keep their airways open. He uses his own handpicked team to care for his critical patients.

After several days, Dr. Harley, who has been reviewing mom's records, decides to see her. That means a trip for Mom and the three of us to San Diego. Janice is still on hospital leave but both Wanda and I are still working and need to arrange to be away for an extended time.

After some wrangling, the County School system, my employer, agrees to give me paid family leave so I can travel to San Diego. Municipal Hospital finances the trip for two sisters on a chartered jet and provides a medical flight for Mom. I catch a commercial flight the next day.

They also agree to provide a rental car and to pay our expenses while we are there. While this was a generous offer, I think the real motivation was to move Mom and the problem she represents from Municipal to the hospital in San Diego.

A Trip to San Diego

Days 181-211

On March 3, Janice and Wanda fly on a Leer jet to San Diego to meet Mom. I followed the next day, buying my own ticket. The hospital told us there was not enough room on the jet for all three of us. Janice told me that the jet was empty but for them. I believe that not allowing all three of us to travel together was a ploy to break us up as a united front. Municipal was worried about a lawsuit from day one. They wanted to make sure that the insurance was paying for all of Mom's care.

The back and forth conversations with Municipal were contentious and added to the discomfort we already felt.

After arriving by medical flight, Mom is admitted to the hospital in San Diego. She has not eaten solid food since September 5.

In these past six months, Mom has endured countless bronchs. Each one takes most of the day, is painful and frightening and takes two days for her to recover.

It has been a constant battle against recurring infections, fevers, pain, and deprivation. Two days before her departure, she started drinking thick liquids. I think this was a last ditch attempt by Municipal to get her stronger so she could survive the trip.

Municipal hospital arranged to give us lodging at the Lancaster House, a high-rise apartment building connected to the hospital, complete with a communal kitchen, lobby, lounge area, and private bedrooms with private baths. There is a well-stocked kitchen, a microwave, and cabinets filled with snacks, cookies, tea bags, and an always-ready coffee dispenser. There was also a huge refrigerator in the shared kitchen so that you could buy food or prepare it and store it in the fridge.

The Lancaster House is a 501(C)(3) charity whose mission is similar to the mission of the Ronald McDonald House in Louisville where families can stay for extended periods while their loved ones recuperate.

What a blessing it was to be able to stay so close to the hospital. Although we don't have a definitive length of stay, they tell us to plan for at least four weeks. The logistics of getting time off work and being in a strange city for an extended period creates a lot of stress.

I remember taking a huge stack of bills from home to be paid while I was in San Diego.

When I arrived at the airport, Janice and Wanda met me along with my cousin Lana who lives in the area. It was helpful to have Lana there to give us some landmarks and direction in San Diego.

San Diego is a beautiful city. I loved the opportunity to see my cousin too, but the emotions of being away from home and dealing with the unknown is getting to all of us.

That first night at Lancaster House, we shared a large bedroom with two double beds, a desk, love seat, two chairs, and a private bath.

When I laid down to sleep, my mind raced. It was full of unanswered questions. I fell asleep praying and asking God, like in the country music song: "Jesus, take the wheel." I was exhausted and more than a little shell-shocked.

One thing I loved about staying at the Lancaster House is the camaraderie of the other visitors. We were all in similar circumstances. All of us had loved ones that were in real trouble medically. Our ability to share our fear, grief, and emotional roller coasters with someone who has "been there, done that" was invaluable. I am so grateful for the wonderful people I met and shared with during our stays at Lancaster House.

Mom is in intensive care. We can only see her at certain times during the day, and then only for short durations. We occupy ourselves by taking breaks between visitations at the hospital café.

After a week, we settled into a comfortable routine, fixing a frozen dinner in the Lancaster House microwave, chatting with other residents, and sometimes even watching a video or a movie in the lounge area. They also have an extensive library. The director of Lancaster House, Marion, gave us a key to the front door so we could come and go as needed, day or night.

On day two, we meet Mom's new doctor, Dr. Harley. He was tall and slim with a commanding, confident, and gentle presence. In his mid-sixties, his salt and pepper hair and beard were the perfect accent to his cowboy boots. His ease and warmth were a stark comparison to the wary and tentative attitudes from the doctors at Municipal.

His smile is welcoming as he says, "I will be installing one of my stents into your mother's airway tomorrow. I believe this will help her. I want you to know that I will do my best for her." As he speaks, one by one, he looks us in the eye.

We exhale a sigh of collective relief as he tells us "not to worry." For the first time in six months, we believe what a medical professional tells us.

The doctors have sedated Mom to allow her to rest after her trip and to be ready for her surgical procedure tomorrow. While she sleeps, we decide to take a short trip in our rental car, guided by our cousin Lana.

We find a beautiful sidewalk café and sit outside to enjoy people watching and the fresh breezes. It is a welcome two hours of respite.

Tomorrow we will find out if Dr. Harley is the cowboy he purports to be.

Mildred Yager, my mother at eighteen years of age.

Aunt Ethel and Mom, ages 6 & 3, photo taken the year that Alice Litsy, their mother, abandoned them.

Mom and her dog at age 12.

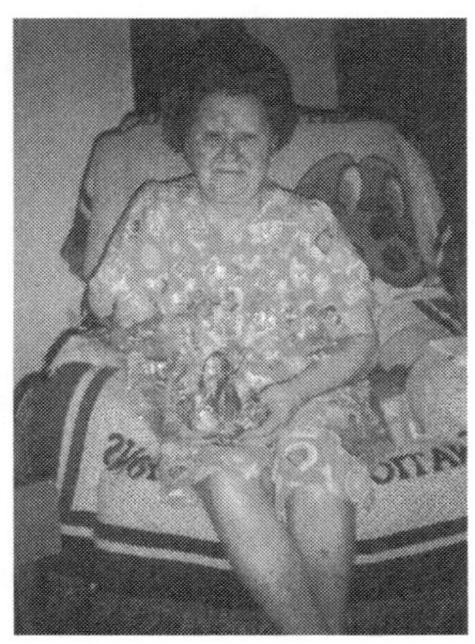

Mom before the Fire and meeting Dr. Robinson.

Jeremy, Jo Ann's son with his grandmother at the hospital in 2000.

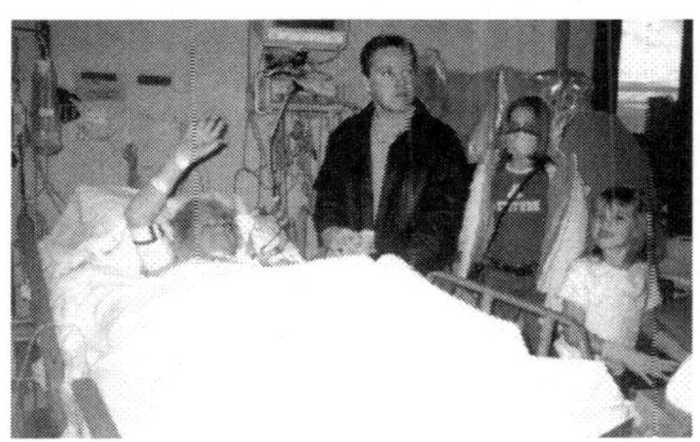

Mom with Jeremy and his daughters, Julia and Miranda, ages 11 and 5. December 2001

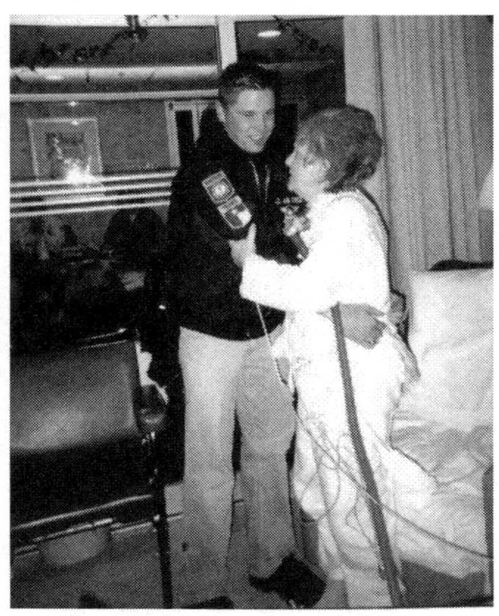

Mom says goodbye to her grandson, Jason (Janice's son) before he leaves for the Air Force.

(left to right) Wanda, Jo Ann, Mom, and Janice on Mother's 75th birthday—complete with 75 balloons.

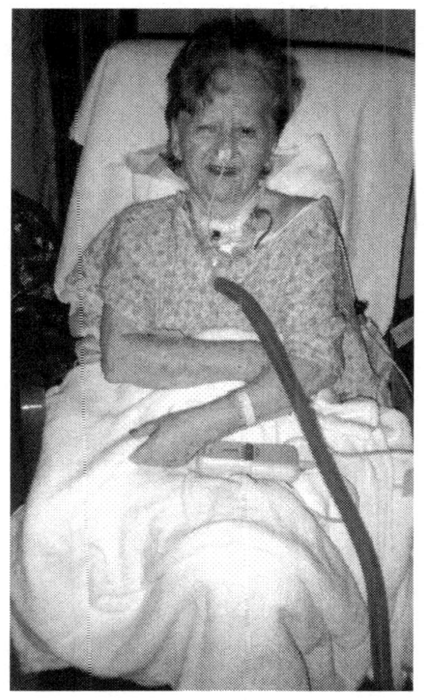

Mom all dolled up in her hospital bed at Municipal Hospital, 2000.

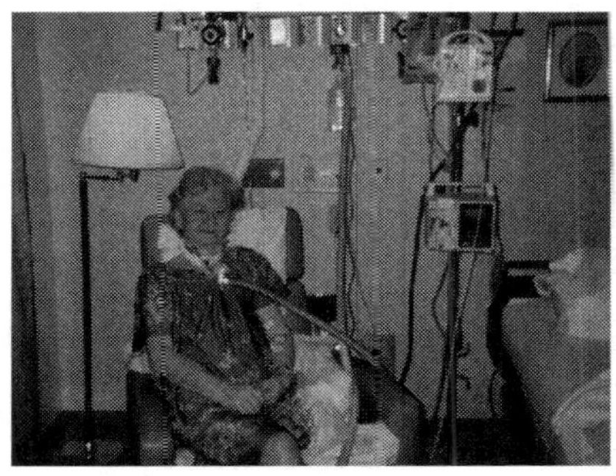

Mom on a good day at Municipal Hospital, 2000.

Leer Jet hired to take us to San Diego. March 2000. This is the flight that the hospital said had no room for me. Janice later told me it was nearly empty.

Return flight from San Diego on Mom's second trip to San Diego, June 2001.
(left to right) Jo Ann, Wanda, and Janice

Lancaster House, where we stayed on all three trips to San Diego

Getting some sunshine for the first time since September 2000 in the hospital cafeteria's outdoor patio in San Diego. Mom, Jo, and Wanda. March 2001

Mom enjoying her first solid food in six months as Jo Ann looks on. This happened on her first visit to San Diego, March 2001.

(left to right) My Aunt Patti, my cousin Lana (Ethel's daughter), and Mom September, 1996

(left to right, back row) Lana, Aunt Patti, Sonny (Ethel's son); Front Row: (left to right) Wanda, me, and Janice

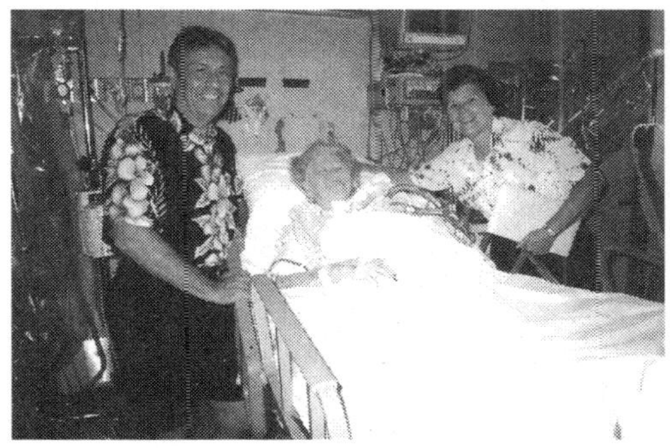

Aunt Pattie and her husband Russ with Mom in the hospital

Taking Mom for a walk in Municipal Hospital, 2000
(left to right) Pattie, Jo Ann, Mom, and Wanda

My husband Jimmy in 2001 celebrating Mom's 75th
birthday

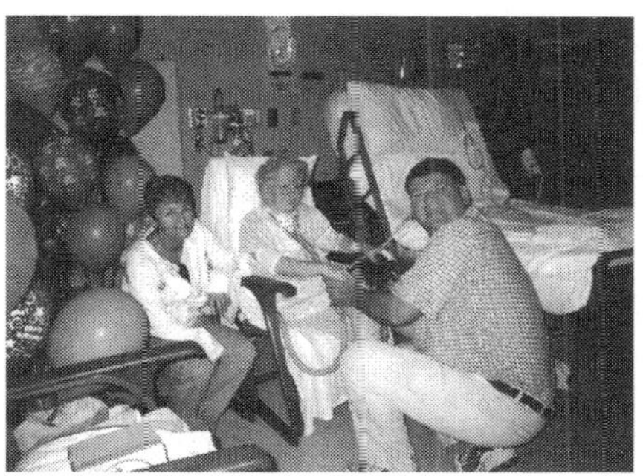

My cousin Sonny kneeling and my sister Wanda with
Mom, Municipal, 2001

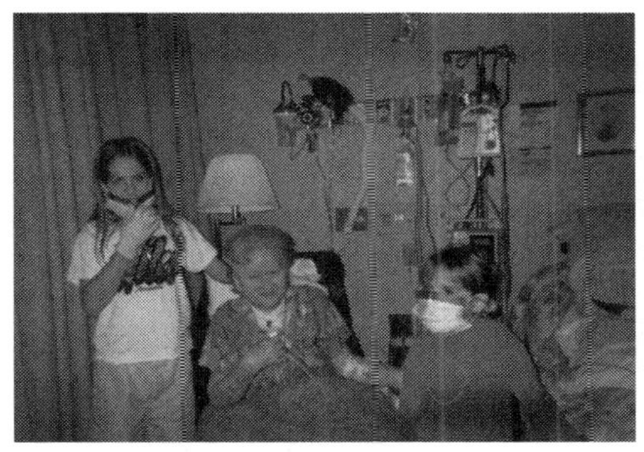

(L to R) Julia, (granddaugher) Mom, and Miranda
(granddaughter), 2001

Mom on our trip to Hawaii in 1989. She was sixty-three years old.

(L to R) Me, Wanda, Mom, and Janice on our ttrip to Hawaii in 1989.

CHAPTER TWELVE

The New Stent and a Respite

Mom is in fine spirits today. She is smiling, despite being tired from her long journey. Dr. Harley is with her and she seems comfortable with him. I think she likes him as much as we do.

After Dr. Harley leaves the room, Mom seems very agitated. She is having trouble breathing again and I am sure she is anxious about the new stent.

Dr. Harley's job is to do everything he can do to prepare her for the procedure. He decides to do two bronchs that day —number 28 … and counting.

"Dr. Harley, Mom seems so anxious today. She seems upset … agitated. Should we be worried?" I wait for the doctor's answer.

"I've seen that look many times before. The eyes always tell the story," he says. "She knows she is having trouble breathing and she most likely knows that means more procedures, whether more bronchs or a stent procedure, both are hard for her. Patients know when they are in trouble. We need to get your Mom as strong as we can before the procedure. My back is against the wall here. Right now, her airway is no bigger than a pinhole. If I can't get a stent installed, she will die. I don't intend to let that happen. Hang in there. She will get better—if we can get her airways open."

He explains exactly what the procedure to install the stent will entail. We feel, maybe for the first time, that the medical community is making an effort to keep us informed and aware of what is happening. I am so grateful to this man for his insight not just in treating my mother, but also in recognizing how left out of the process we have been.

Dr. Kimber, one of Dr. Harley's handpicked team, uses a balloon on Mom's throat to force the airway open. Afterwards, she is back on the ventilator, but it seems to give her a chance to rest. She falls asleep immediately.

Mom's lungs are slowly filling with fluid. As they fill, she feels more pressure and less ability to get her breath. I want this procedure to be done.

I say a silent prayer. *God, please help her ... help us all. Bless the work of Dr. Harley's hands. Amen.*

Journal Entry:
March 10, 2001

We wait in the hallway while Dr. Harley tries to open her airway enough to get a new stent installed. The process takes nearly two hours. Dr. Harley walks out and talks to us. "I was able to open the airway enough to install the stent. Your Mom is sleeping. She most likely will sleep most of the day."

We have waited six months for a ray of sunshine to come into our lives and this is it. Dr. Harley feels good about being able to insert the stent. He tells us her airways are deeply scarred, but despite that, the stent is in place. He thinks her breathing will be much easier moving forward.

Back in her room, she is awake for a moment and we give her the good news. We also get to tell her that later today she will get a plate of real food!

Her eyes sparkle like fireworks at a Fourth of July picnic. I share with her the good news Dr. Harley has given us. 'Around here, we feed our patients real food. You can expect a real meal delivered tonight for supper.'

We all laughed. It was the first real laugh I had allowed myself to have since Christmas Day.

When they brought   Mom a plate of food, I thought she would jump out of bed she was so happy. At Municipal, they had always been afraid to feed her. Afraid she would choke.

I removed the domed lid covering her supper. She had mashed potatoes, carrots, and fried chicken. The smell alone sent her into ecstasy. Her eyes took it all in, skating from white creamy potatoes to fiery orange carrots and finally to the savory chicken. For us it was run-of-the-mill "hospital food" but for Mom, who had not eaten a bite of solid food for over six months, it was heaven on a plate.

She picked up her fork, raised it to us in salute, and took her first bite of solid food in over six months. She was smiling so wide. The tiny bite rested in her mouth, when she swallowed it seemed to warm her from the inside out. A bite of carrots, then potatoes again. She never made it to the chicken—she was already full. The look on her face said it all. Pure contentment. I can still see those smiling eyes.

Overall, the weeks spent in San Diego are filled with tiny victories every day. She feels better and the solid food makes her happy.

Our routine consists of helping her eat a few bites for breakfast, then a nap while we go grab a fresh cup of coffee and some breakfast in the cafeteria.

At lunchtime, she eats a few bites of solid food, but the feeding tube, still in her stomach, is always the main source of nutrition. After lunch, another nap before dinner.

She watches television a little, but falls asleep easily. Because we are at Lancaster House, we feel comfortable walking back to our rooms after supper and relaxing a little. It is such a comfort to know that if the nurses call we can be back in Mom's room in minutes. I think Mom feels safer knowing we are close by all the time and that Dr. Harley and the hospital staff are there for her if she needs anything.

Although Mom is still in intensive care, she is often sitting up in bed when we see her in the mornings. She still has good times and bad, good days and bad. Overall, I would say the good times are beginning to outweigh the bad.

We know if she's had a bad night because she will be on the ventilator when we walk in. Infections are the bane of her existence. The slightest infection can throw her back to the ventilator. They crash her energy level and her spirit.

Journal Entries:

March 18, 2001

Dr. Kimberly comes in to check on Mom. He tells us that she will always require suctioning. "Her airways are so restricted," she says. "This will always be required. She was suctioned all night last night."

Her recurring eye infection is back. Mom is tired. There is little chance to sleep because they are suctioning through most of the night.

I think she is depressed, again. This is such a roller coaster ride. I never get used to walking into her room and wondering if today will be a good day or a terrible day. Will there be smiles or tears? This week, one of us stays with her twenty-four hours a day.

March 23, 2001

The current stent in Mom's airways is a number 12. When it comes to stents, the bigger the better. Dr. Harley's team comes in every day to check on her progress. We are still staying with her on a 24-hour basis. We take turns spending the night. The eye infection is better but still seems to be a problem.

Dr. Harley comes to her room to check her three times per day. The feeding tube continues to supply the bulk of her nutrition. Today Mom told me she has been in the hospital too long. "Want to go home," she mouths.

We continue our stay at Lancaster House. On the weekends, Lana comes to see us and we sneak away for a few hours to see the city or grab a bite to eat that hasn't been prepared by a hospital. It helps us so much to get out in the sun. Until you have been sheltered inside a hospital for weeks on end, you don' realize how much you miss the sun- shine.

Lately, Mom has been strong enough to sit outside in the cafeteria area on warm afternoons. I have to believe that just feeling the warmth of the sun on her skin is healing.

Journal Entry:

March 31, 2001

Dr. Harley tells us that we are

heading home and back to Municipal

Hospital. Mom is better than she has been since this nightmare began. I wonder how long we can keep the progress going once we are back in Louisville. My confidence is not high.

I leave first, Janice, Wanda, and Mom will leave a day behind me. It has been a tough six weeks for my husband. When you walk away from your life for several weeks, things don't get done. Bills are piling up, taxes need filing—life doesn't have a pause button. I wish it did.

CHAPTER THIRTEEN

Back to Municipal:

Days 212-240
Five days later, and multiple phone calls by Janice and Dr. Harley, Municipal Hospital sends a jet to fly Mom and my sitters back home. Dr. Harley thinks it is best that Municipal take over her care now that she is better.

I am not so sure. However, Mom seems ready and anxious to be back home, even though she will still be hospitalized.

April 4, 200 1

Scott Thursney the RN from Air Response is in charge of mom's care on the flight back home. During the   trip,   Mom begins having trouble breathing even with the help of a respirator. Sweat beads on her forehead. Her breathing is strained. Scott seems worried about her condition but she seems to stabilize. Once the plane lands, a Municipal Hospital ambulance is waiting for her where she is admitted to intensive care. They tell us she has fluid on her lungs but she has a peaceful night.

Mom spends the next few days visiting with family and friends. Many of Janice's friends and staff at the hospital also stop by to check on her.

Dr. Harley calls to see how she is doing. He is disappointed that the flight back took such a toll on her but glad to hear that she is holding her own.

There is a change of atmosphere as we settle back into Municipal Hospital. The doctors and nursing staff seem more distant. Are they tired of caring for a patient who is not getting better? When faced with the chronically sick, nursing staff and doctors alike can develop a kind of caregiver fatigue. Not unlike the frustration and sometimes even resentment that can settle into caregivers who are tired, stressed, and almost hopeless in the face of relentless illness.

It's nothing specific, but more a general malaise on the part of the nursing staff.

Sadly, we sense the hospital really doesn't want Mom back. The body language is different and the care is much more automatic without any kind of interaction except when necessary.

I think Mom is aware of the change too. God, I hope she is not. She doesn't need the staff giving up on her.

Journal Entry:
April 5, 200 1

It's mom's 75th birthday. Janice wants to bring 75 balloons to her room. She talks to the head nurse on Mom's floor to give her a heads -up. "Janice," the head nurse s ays, "I don't think that's a good idea. You should probably not do that."

"Watch me." Janice is adamant. "There are no 'balloon rules,'" she says. We busy ourselves buying a small helium canister and set about filling 75 balloons. It took three cars to get them to the hospital.

When Mom woke up the following morning, her room was filled with 75 colorful balloons. She was thrilled. It was worth all the sore fingers tying those balloon knots. It was a wonderful day. She had loads of visitors, family and friends dotted the chairs. At times, there was standing room only between visitors and balloons.

Journal Entry:

April 9, 200 1

Mom tests positive for VRE (Vancomycin-resistant enterococci). VRE is anti-biotic resistant. The   bacteria normally live in the intestines and on our skin without causing a problem. When the immune system is compromised (as Mom's system was), it can proliferate and spark an infection anywhere in the body. Sadly, most VRE infections occur in hospitals.

We talk to Dr. Kara   when he comes to see her. We tell him that we have been staying with mom 24-7 since this infection. Th is area of the hospital has seven patients to one nurse. He agrees to get an aide to stay with her so we can go home and get some rest. We urge him to move her back to VCU where the nurse to patient ratio is half what it is here.

It has been seven months since the Fire. I honestly don't know how Mom does it. Day after day, she puts on a strong face. But deep in her eyes, I can see the fear and the deep sadness.

One afternoon, while we are alone, I ask her for the first time since this started, "Mom, have you had enough?" She looks at me, and smiles a knowing smile. "No," she mouths the words to me. "I want you to tell them my story." She says, barely a whisper.

"You want me to tell your story? Is that what you are saying?"

"Yes, tell my story. Help someone."

I look into her eyes and promise her, "I will tell them your story, Mom. I promise you. I will tell them."

She seems relieved. She turns her head and sighs. As I watch her sleep, I wonder how I will keep my promise.

Journal Entry:

April 18, 200 1

Dr. Timothy does bronch number 32. We get lucky. He is able to dilate both of her airways.

CHAPTER FOURTEEN

Legal Dis-ease

There is so much going on. In the midst of it, there are the unavoidable legal and financial hassles that never seem to go away. Mr. Royel, our attorney, tells us it will be months or years before our case is settled.

Journal Entry:

April 18, 2001

Janice gets a call from Melanie Updrake, legal liaison for Municipal Hospital. Our conversation is tense and adversarial.

"Why didn't you tell me y   ou are represented by an attorney? I was told in a meeting that you have hired Larry Royel to represent you. I can no longer meet with you. You should have let us know you have hired an attorney. I really don't know what to do or say about this situation."

Janice is incredulous. "You really need to put yourself in our situation."

"'I've tried to do that, Janice."

Janice felt that Melanie was trying to make her feel guilty, as though she had betrayed her in some way.

"Look, Melanie, I am only trying to look out for Mom and for all of us in this mess."

"Janice, it's not like we are going to throw your mother out of the hospital."

"Melanie, do you hear what you are saying? Really? This is absurd. Do you have any inkling of the pain, stress, and worry that my mother and our family have endured these past seven months? I think our family has been cordial considering the circumstances. I think we have behaved well, far better than other families may have behaved under these same circumstances."

Melanie is silent for several seconds. "All that being said, Janice, I think you should have let us know."

"Consider yourself informed," Janice told her.

Dr. Harley calls and wants Municipal to fly Mom back to San Diego in June in order to follow up with her treatment. He feels that our attorney will make sure we don't have any hassles about a return flight to San Diego at Municipal's expense. I hope he is right.

CHAPTER FIFTEEN

A Brief Trip Home

Days 241-272

Suddenly, the nursing staff seems bent on teaching us how to do daily suctioning on Mom's trach. I'm not sure why, but I suspect that the insurance may be running out.

Suctioning doesn't always require inserting a tube into the lungs, but in Mom's case, it means clearing the throat of mucus and detritus. It is an uncomfortable procedure for Mother and an unsettling one for us to perform.

This is the first time I have done the suctioning and I am nervous. First, I gather my supplies and make sure I have everything I need: a suction machine, connecting tubing, disinfected suction catheter, a non-sterile clean glove, distilled water, and a clean paper cup.

I wash my hands carefully with soap and water and put on the latex glove. Next, I fill the small paper cup half-full with distilled water. Next, I open the catheter package. I attach the catheter tubing to the connective tubing. I am careful to wrap the excess tubing around my gloved hand to keep it from being contaminated. With my un-gloved hand, I turn on the suction and open the tracheostomy opening.

I place the tube in the opening and slowly ad-vance the tubing about six inches or until I feel a slight resistance. Once the tube is in place, I cover the trach opening with the thumb of my ungloved hand. This will create a vacuum and causes the machine to begin suctioning. Now I roll the suc-tion tube between my thumb and index finger of my gloved hand. *It is critical that the suction is never applied for more than 10 seconds.*The nurses never tell me why the suction should not exceed ten seconds, but because they emphasize it, I am terrified I will make a mistake and harm my mother.

Once I'm done, the tubing must be rinsed and the process begins again. I give Mom 30 seconds to recover from the last clearing and I begin again. I look at her face between suctioning and I see the worry and empathy in her eyes. This is such a difficult and frightening exercise for us both.

After three repetitions, I feel her airway is clear and I remove all equipment, clean the tubing and put things away. I am exhausted. My polyester blouse sticks to my underarms. I am overwhelmed by the experience but don't want Mom to know how much it has upset me.

We are both done in. Gratefully, she falls asleep. I don't know if this is something I can do every two hours once my mother is at home.

Janice, Wanda, and I have all done the clearing procedure one time. None of us feels comfortable with it. The nurses are anxious for us to embrace the idea and are irritated when we ask questions. I don't like how this is going. They have all done this hundreds if not thousands of times, and we have done it once.

Later that afternoon, Janice gets a phone call from Cindy Gaylord, Dr. Kara's nurse.

"Janice, I wanted to let you know that the doctor is planning to discharge your mom this Friday, May 5."

"Cindy, are you kidding? I don't think that's a good idea. We have only suctioned Mom one time. We just don't feel comfortable at all being on our own with her. That will be Derby eve, not the best day to have her riding in an ambulance to go home."

After Janice hangs up, she calls Dr. Kara and asks if he can come by Mom's room to talk with us regarding her release. We don't see him until late in the day.

"Dr. Kara, are you seriously considering releasing Mom so soon? I don't think we are ready or adequately trained to take care of Mom without much more training or professional help. Are you aware that there is blood coming out of her nose and that there are bloody secretions from the last bronch? Are you sure she is ready to be discharged?"

"Janice, the blood is nothing to worry about. She will get better at home."

"Look, Dr. Kara, I don't agree. I think she needs the professional care she gets here, in the hospital."

The doctor hesitates before he answers. After a few seconds, he says, "Look Janice, the reality is that the insurance won't pay anymore. If she gets home and gets into trouble, you can bring her right back. Her insurance will kick in and she will be re-admitted. I hate that it has come to this, but it's out of my hands. I'm sorry."

There is nothing we can do. Our new reality. The hospital won't keep Mom unless they have assurances that her medical bills are covered.

Journal Entry:

May 5, 2001

Dr. Salon is on call. She examines Mom and says she "thinks" she will be okay to discharge. I don't believe her. I don't believe any of them. This is about money, not care. My confidence and respect for these "medical professionals" is shattered.

After eight grueling months in the hospital, Mom is going home. They pack her into the front seat of Janice's car and say goodbye

She is going home whether she is strong enough or not. My heart is pounding as I drive to Mom's house. I can't imagine how s cared Janice must be. Mom is fragile and we have no idea how hard it will be on her. Because Mom has a trach, the ride is rough. It's Derby eve and the traffic is building. Janice pulls into Mom's driveway shortly after 6 pm.

Lord, help us to get through this.

By the time we arrive home, Mom is four hours overdue to be suctioned. We have arranged for the visiting nurses to meet us at the house. They are scheduled to be there ahead of our arrival, setup all the suctioning equipment and help us suction the first time at home.

When I pull into the driveway, the visiting nurses are not there. We decide to get Mom into the house and get her settled while we wait for them to show up.

Once inside, we put Mom in her favorite recliner. She hasn't been home for months. This should be a joyous moment for all of us but instead, Mom is struggling to breath, and we are terrified the nurses aren't going to get here.

Janice gives Mom some water and a couple of crackers. I still have not filled all Mom's prescriptions so I run to the drugstore to take care of that while Janice and Wanda tend to Mom. There were eight prescriptions in all so I was gone for about 45 minutes. When I get home, she is gone. Everyone is gone!

I realize that they must have taken Mom back to the hospital. I immediately head to Municipal. I find Janice in the emergency room and she tells me what happened while I was at the drugstore.

"Jo, it was awful. Mom began wheezing badly. I ask her if she was okay. Her lips were turning blue. I tell her to hold on because someone is at the door. I am praying it is the visiting nurse. Instead, it is a courier delivering the suctioning supplies. Desperate for help, I beg him, 'Please, I need your help. My Mom is suffocating. She's turning blue. Can you help me get her into the car? Please … I think she is dying.'"

"Oh, my God, Janice. How did you ever get her back here in time?" I asked.

"It wasn't easy. Mom was gasping for air. Her whole face was turning blue. I was driving like a maniac. The traffic was worse than on the trip from the hospital. Jo, I was driving 50 mph down the emergency lane on the expressway. Once we arrived, the ER staff took her out of the car and loaded her onto a gurney. I can honestly sa y that was the worst ride of my life."

"I'm sorry, Janice. Thank God, you got her back here in time. How is she?"

"Jo, by the time I got here she was unresponsive."

A few minutes later, as we waited in the emergency room, they called us back to Mom's area. The respiratory nurse tells us that she was able to extract a "mucus plug" that was blocking Mom's airway. He pulled the trach out completely. Dr. Mayfield and Dr. Nursing are going to do the emergency bronch.

They clear her airways, insert trach number six and put her on a ventilator. Mom is sleeping.

After everything has settled down, Janice allows herself to feel the anxiety that she has been denying herself for the past several hours. She begins to quietly sob, her shoulders shaking, her head in her hands. I put my arm around her and

say, "You know, Janice, you saved Mom's life today. You saved her life."

CHAPTER SIXTEEN

Back at Municipal

Mom is back at Municipal after her four -hour stay at home. She is still on the ventilator and lucky to be alive after nearly suffocating on the ride with Janice back to the hospital.

She is scheduled for bronch, number 34.

Journal Entry:

May 8, 2001

Dr. Timothy and Dr. Tara do a successful bronch. Finally, they take her off the ventilator. She is exhausted and feeling down. Who could blame her?

The feeding tube is still supplying all of her nutrition. I think eating a meal again would cheer her but that doesn't seem to be in the offing. Maybe when we go to San Diego. I find myself counting the days until she is back in the care of Dr. Harley and his team.

Since Mom was re-admitted, Janice has had several opportunities to speak with the nurses and other staff members about the mandatory release and re-admittance.

While we are in the room waiting for Mom's doctor to check on her, I asked Janice how she feels about the nurses and staff after the harrowing hours during Mom's short home visit.

"Jo, I had a conversation with Dr. Timothy yesterday. I told him right up front. 'You know that Mom nearly died on Friday because of a mucus plug. That one-day discharge nearly killed her."

"What did Dr. Timothy say to that comment?" I asked.

"He said he was very sorry about that discharge but that his 'hands were tied.' The good news is that he told me he would not feel good about discharging her at all moving forward. At least we have some peace of mind on that front."

The next day I was visiting with Mom when Dr. Parado came in. He examined Mom then looked at me for a moment, pausing before he spoke. I was shocked to hear him say, "You know, Jo Ann, I would never have allowed your mother to be discharged while she was having bloody secretions. I had no idea this was happening."

Journal Entry:

May 11, 2001

The one-day discharge has taken quite a toll. She now has multiple infections: MRSA, VRE, and ESBL. All of which are tough to defeat and are anti-biotic resistant. These infections are generally hospital acquired. I am concerned that Mom has started down a road from which she may never return.

We also get a call from Dr. Harley. He says the mucus plug is more reason to see her back in San Diego and have a larger stent installed. I am so glad to hear his voice. It is like a warm water bath after a cold day outside.

Dr. Harley is not happy with the Mom's treatment at Municipal. Neither am I but we are powerless to do anything else. I am so overwhelmed at this point that all I do is cry myself to sleep and say multiple daily prayers for all of us. How Mom has survived all of this is a miracle. I wonder where she finds the strength.

I asked her again last night, "Mom, have you had enough?"

"No," she whispered. "No."

CHAPTER SEVENTEEN

San Diego—Again

Days 273-332

We are scheduled to take Mom back to San Diego on June 4. My hope is that Municipal will pay without objection for our transportation. I am not convinced that they won't hassle us again.

The hospital case manager; Debra Pitts calls to "discuss" the trip to San Diego.

Debra is a heavy-set woman with blond hair, sharp blue eyes and a strictly business disposition.

I'm not sure if she saves that just for us, or she is always that way with people. She begins the meeting with a statement of position.

"Thank you all for coming. Jo, Janice, I appreciate your being here. As you know, the hospital's position on this second trip to San Diego is fine, but we (the hospital) feel that you should pay your own expenses, including the air ambulance. The hospital is aware that you have hired a lawyer and that a malpractice suit may be forthcoming. Because of that decision, the hospital feels you should be prepared to pay for the transportation yourselves.

Debra told Janice earlier that had it been her mother she would have quit her job in order to focus on my mother's care. Was that her way of telling Janice she should resign from her job at Municipal rather than ask for a leave of absence? What a nerve.

Debra continues, "Let me say, right up front, unless you tell me who your attorney is, I will not continue to talk with you. I believe that Larry Royel is your attorney, and I need to contact our hospital attorney to get approval to send your mother back to San Diego. You really should get Dr. Robinson to pay for this, not Municipal."

We are shocked to hear her say this in front of everyone attending the meeting.

Eventually our attorney makes contact with the Municipal attorney. They are wrangling over who will pay for Mom's transport to San Diego. In the meantime, Mom grows weaker. I am concerned that all anyone cares about is the money. This is no longer a human interaction, but a financial one.

Dr. Kara, Dr. Timothy, and Dr. Harley have all sent letters to the administration expressing their concern that Mom be transported to San Diego for advanced treatment. At last, after a week of negotiation the trip is approved. Mom is schedule to leave for San Diego on June 4, 2001.

Once in San Diego, Dr. Harley successfully installs a larger stent. He shares with us that Mom's case is the worst he has ever seen. He is amazed that she is still fighting. We take this comment seriously. It comes from a pulmonary physician who has been treating patients for over thirty years.

We stay at Lancaster House again on this trip. What a blessing.

On June 8, we travel back home and back to Municipal. Mom has a rough trip. She suffers several panic attacks. I can't help but believe that knowing she is going back to Municipal is frightening to her. She has had so many negative experiences there. Once back in Louisville, Mom is in VCU where they can suction her and take care of her trach. Dr. Harley has scheduled a third trip to San Diego at the end of July. We are planning that trip when Dr. Kara comes in one day to examine Mom and says, "I hear something in her right lung. I think it may be the stent. She should go back to San Diego and have Dr. Harley check that stent. She needs to go back as soon as possible."

This time, everyone is supportive of helping us transport our mother back to San Diego. They arrange the flight without any hassle and tell us that 'there is no guarantee that they will pay for a return flight.'

It all seems too easy. It is as if they don't want Mom here. Are they hoping to transfer the 'burden' of her care to Dr. Harley? I keep wondering why Mom's third trip to San Diego has been expedited. Then I get a call from Debra, the case manager.

Journal Entry:

June 27, 2001

Debra Pitts calls to tell me that Mom's insurance is run ning out. She tells me we will be getting a letter   from the hospital informing us that Mom either needs to go home and have us take re-sponsibility for her care or put her in a nursing home.

Now I understand the urgency to get her out of Municipal and into the San Diego system. Now she is, from their perspective, San Diego's headache and not theirs.

I am shocked at the state of medical care in our system. We don't realize it, but we are on ra-tioned care. If you are too old or too sick or can't self-pay, then it's better frcm the "systems" per-spective that you die. We live in a world where you get the medical care you can afford. I hate making that statement, but it's true. I have lived it.

As the days pass, Dr. T mothy manages to sta-bilize Mom.

Journal Entries:
June 29, 2001

Dr. Timothy does bronch number 38. He manages to dilate both bronch stems. The number 14 stent looks good. He tells us she will need suctioning on a regular basis as before. Her eye infection is better but not gone. There is a new wrinkle —she has to be dilated every two weeks.

July 4, 2001

We met with Dr. Kara today. He is insisting we go back to San Diego for the third time. What a shock. At first, they resist all trips to San Diego, now they insist. What is going on?

He says he is still hearing a noise in her right lung. I am shocked to hear him tell us that Dr. Robinson lacked the training and credenti aling required to use the laser. We had heard this already, but to have it verified by her new doctor was disturbing.

He insists that we take Mom back
to San Diego. It may be a one-way trip.
I wonder if Dr. Kara believes that too.
If he does, he doesn't say so.

July 9, 2001

After several phone calls between
our attorney, Municipal, Dr. Kara and
Dr. Harley, Mom is on her way to San
Diego.

We pack as best we can without knowing how
long we will be there. Janice, Wanda and I leave on
July 5, to meet Mom at the hospital in San   Diego.
All of us have a certain dread of this trip but we
soldier on in hopes that Dr. Harley can help.

Back in San Diego, Dr. Harley examines Mom.
We are grateful to hear that her stent is fine. He
wants to remove that stent and insert a larger one
to help with her breathing. Mom is slow to recover
after the surgery. She is lethargic. Dr. Harley has
her moved to ICU. Her stats are dropping. Cardi-
ology calls in V -tack to shock her heart back into

rhythm. In less than a minute, the room is full of doctors and nurses.

Journal Entries:
July 15, 2001
We sit together in the waiting room as the doctor tells us Mom has blood in her trach.

July 16, 2001.
Dr. Harley does bronch number 39. He removes blood clots from the trach and pulls 1.5 liters of fluid from her right lung. They place a Swan-Ganz catheter in her neck to measure heart pressure. The afternoon's chest x-ray shows more fluid in her lungs. She is sedated. We wait and we cry.

July 17, 2001
Dr. Harley removes another 1.5 liters of fluid.

July 20, 2001

Dr. Harley does bronch number 40.
Mom looks pale and fragile. She is exhausted. She needs to be strong for her
stent procedure on Wednesday but she
is still on antibiotics.

Over the next few days, Mom   is trending
downward. We are depressed and feeling helpless.
I talk to our attorney, but he is really no help. One
thing you learn in these situations, very few people
are in a position to help you emotionally. Doctors
hate losing patients and are not inclined to deal
with the aftermath.

In Mom's case, she was here because of medical malpractice. Even though it wasn't Dr. Harley
that made the mistake, it is still a black mark on
his profession. I feel that makes it much harder for
medical professionals to discuss any of the emotions the family is feeling.

If I were ever in this position again, and I hope
to God that I never am —I would recommend that
the hospital pay for a therapist.   I think having
someone to talk to that wasn't involved in the case
and could be objective would have helped us better

cope. It makes me wonder why the nurses received counseling on the same day as the Fire, yet the family received none.

By August 6, Mom is strong enough to sit up in a chair. However, she is still accumulating fluid in her lungs, and her heartbeat is still erratic from the stress of the extra fluid on her lungs.

It is not an easy time. Mom appreciates the care she is receiving in San Diego. Even though, she is getting weaker, the doctors tell me every day that she is a living miracle. I hope Mom feels some encouragement from their observations.

Dr. Harley arranged for us to return home on August 17. I am hopeful she is strong enough to make the trip one more time. We have been in San Diego for seven weeks. It is hard to believe I have been gone from my home and my job for such a long time.

The school where I work is saving my job for me. They have been so generous. When faced with a medical crisis, we never stop to think of the ramifications. Janice, Wanda and I are grateful that we have been able to be with Mom through this ordeal. I think our family is stronger for it.

I spoke with Mom again today, the day before we leave to go back home, "Mom, have you had enough?"

She looks at me and with a weak smile, she mouths the words, "the story …continues …no …I have not had enough."

I believe her. If she can take it, so can I. That thought helps me make it through another day.

On our last day in San Diego, Dr. Harley stops by to tell us that Mom will be back with him in October. My thought is *will she be strong enough to make a fourth trip?*

CHAPTER EIGHTEEN

Rollercoaster: Days 333-498

Days 333-498

We have been gone for nine weeks. When Mom is re-admitted to Municipal, there are no beds in VCU so she is put in a room on the fifth floor. The nurses in this unit don't have experience with trach patients. We make sure there is someone with her all the time.

After a good deal of negotiation, Mom is transferred to VCU where she can be properly monitored.

Journal Entries:
August 24, 2001

Mom is tired and her blood pressure is low. Dr. Savor wants to do a catheter on Tuesday. She is perspiring. Dr. Kara thinks it may be her heart. She has lost more weight and is weak. She weighs 140 pounds. I wonder if she has bleeding internally.

August 28, 2001

Mom receives two units of blood and has an EGD done. In thisprocedure, the blood vessels in the abdomen are cauterized to stop bleeding. Afterward she is on the ventilator most of the night.

September 11, 2001

I am on leave from work so I can spend more time with Mom during this intense period of rehabilitation and healing. It is very early on September 11, 2001. The morning of the infamous attack on the World Trade Center, 9/11.

I was dressed and in my car, driving to the hospital. I usually don't listen to the radio when I drive. For me it is a distraction.

When I get to the hospital, I see Mom glued to the television set. She can't really "see" the TV, maybe a shadow here or there, but her hearing is still fine. Pictures of the smoking towers of the World Trade Center assault my eyes.

There is fire and smoke. I see people's faces covered in a white powder. Debris is everywhere. As I continue to watch, I see the second tower fall, as in a controlled demolition, it collapses in on itself.

I can't believe this is happening to our country. There is talk of a terrorists attack. Next, we hear a hi-jacked plane has crash-landed, then the Pentagon is attacked. Can this be happening?

It is a powerful metaphor for what is happening to my family. Mom seems mesmerized by the events that are unfolding. My heart pounds as they show the devastation.

The tears are flowing down Mom's checks. She nods her head slightly as if to say, "why now ... why this?" We don't talk. There is a lot of nonverbal communication. We just sit near each other and cling to the comfort that provides both of us.

September 13, 2001

Dr. Kara does bronch number 4   1. Mom has a lot of mucus   plugs, which Dr. Kara is able to remove. It is a beautiful fall day. I would love to take Mom outside, but she is in VCU   and that is not possible.

I ask her one more time, "Mo m, how are you doing? Have you had enough?" I had to know.

"No," she mouths. "Not yet."

September 21, 2001

The doctors do bronch 42 and 43.

September 26, 2001

They have the results of Mom's CT scan. Janice isn't here right now so Dr. Kara talked to me. "Your mother has mediastinitis."

"What does that mean?" I asked.

"She has inflammation of the outside of the lung and the sternum. The only way we can relieve it is to do surgery. She can't handle that. She isn't strong enough."

"What can we do?"

"We need to make her a no code. Do not resuscitate. Look, Jo Ann, if we do CPR on her, it will tear her up. She's too weak and it will do more damage and most likely won't work. We need to make her as DNR (Do Not Resuscitate) right now."

"Dr. Kara, I can't make that decision right now. I need time. I need to speak with Janice and Wanda."

"Maybe I can give Janice a call right now?"

I can't believe this is happening, but I tell him I will call her now. When she answers, I hand the phone over to Dr. Kara. He explains the situation to Janice just as he did with me.

Janice decides to get a second opinion and she tells Dr. Kara that she

wants to speak with Mom's other doctors before making this decision.

We tell Dr. Kara that for tonight, no
decision regarding a DNR will be made.

As it turns out, Mom's condition improved
steadily during the night so a no-code decision be-
comes irrelevant. For now.

Journal Entry:
September 30, 2001
We speak with Dr. Harley by phone
regarding the mediastinitis. He believes
the metal stent that was original inserted by Dr. Robinson and could never be
removed is the source of the problem.
He believes it could possibly be working
its way through the scar tissue.

Things seem to settle down into a tense normal.
Nothing has been "normal" since the Fire, but at
least it is quiet with no active crisis.

I feel that the doctors and nurses want to be rid
of the "problem" of our family and my mother's
care. It seems she has less frequent visits from the

medical staff. This is worrisome . We decide to rotate staying with Mom 24 hours a day. Mom's rate of infection is getting more intense. The hospital transfers her to the fourth floor to monitor the latest infection. She grows weaker, more fragile.

We have become effective at using body language and facial expressions to communicate with Mom. She is exhausted. I know that, but I sense she has not given up ...not just yet.

Journal Entries:
October 6, 2001

Someone calls a code 300 for room 405, which means someone has stopped breathing. Mom's room is 408. During the code, there were two nursin g assistants in Mom's room, but no nurses.

After the one nursing assistant leaves, Mom's ventilator comes off. The nursing assistant has pulled Mom's curtains shut. Because of this, the assistant does not see that the vent is off.

A moment later one of th e RNs comes by, walks deeper into the room and seesthat Mom is unresponsive. Dr.

Martin comes into the room and calls for a crash cart. They apply 100% oxygen. Mom revives and smiles at Dr. Martin.

We find out that Mary Jane, the nursing assistant, was disciplined.

No one from the hospital called to tell us what had happened. We learned about it later that day. A truly appalling lack of empathy with the patient's family.

October 7, 2001

I tell Mary Jane, the disciplined nursing assistant that we are not feeling safe right now. She apologizes to all of us and assures us that Mom's care is top priority for her and for the rest of the staff.

Mom doesn't recognize one of her regular nurses. Her stats are dropping and things look bad. She sweats a lot. We suspect it is her heart again.

November 17, 2001

When I walked into mom's room to-night, she d idn't' recognize me. I am heart broken and scared. Her blood sugars are 24 and she is sweating again. Blood sugars are becoming harder to control.

December 7, 2001

Mom is off the ventilator for the first time in a while. She still doesn't know who I am. I ask the nurse to put her back on the vent. When Amy, the RN suctions her, bright red blood comes out.

December 14, 2001

Janice comes into Mom's room after work to check on her. She is slumped over in a chair. She was nearly on the floor. We suspect she had been sitting there a long time and gradually slipped down and wasn't able to pull herself up again. She may have been unconscious. We see this as a sign of d eteriorating care. Someone should have checked on her. When Janice tried to pull her back into the chair, Mom was covered in sweat.

The nurses checked her sugars. They were 36. Janice asked a few pointed questions and discovers that her assigned nurse was busy with another patient and hadn't checked on her for a while.

"That is not acceptable," Janice told the nurse. "She is in an intensive care unit. Neglect is not an option here." Mary Jane shows up to ask what happened. She assures us, again, that this won't happen anymore. I tell them all that the curtain is to be open at all times moving forward.

December 25, 2001

It's Christmas day and Mom is putting on a good face but she is very sick. We go over all the cards she received and she has a couple of v   isitors. She can't have too many visitors . She is too weak. We make the best of it.

2002

January 7, 2002

Mom is unresponsive. Her bilirubin
is high. Not good. I am beyond exhausted. I can only imagine what Mom must
be feeling.

CHAPTER NINETEEN

The Final Challenge

It is January 9, 2002. A brand new year is beginning and I am exhausted. T he roller coaster we have been riding for sixteen months is nearing its end. We have begun a long decent into falling stats, broken spirits, and deep fatigue.

Although Mom continues to put on a brave face, we are losing her. I have never seen anyone die. I'm not sure what to look for but I feel in my bones that my mother is dying.

Like so much in life that is important and relevant to our lives, seeing my mother pass from this life into the next is the most important thing I can observe.

It is early morning on January 9 and Mom is asleep when I walk into the room. She sleeps nearly all the time now.

One of her nurses walks into the room to get the latest stats; blood pressure, pulse. As she makes notes and watches the monitors, she begins to talk to me. "You know Jo Ann; I wanted you to know that last night your Mom told me she was 'ready to go.' We really should put her on a morphine drip. You should consider turning everything off."

I ponder this alleged conversation between the medical attendant and my mother. Mom would never have said, 'I am ready to go'. She would have said, "I've had enough."

In my heart, I believed that this 'conversation' had never taken place. I remained silent for a few seconds more, and then replied, "What do you mean 'turn everything off'? Morphine is an end-of-life thing. It is to make the patient comfortable while they die. No, we are not ready to do that. No"

They are ready for her to be gone. It hits me hard, but I have to face the facts. Their reluctance to prolong her life is obvious. I   am heartbroken.

Scared. How could I possibly make a life and death decision for Mom?

I listened to chatter about ending Mom's life, but I said nothing further. As I silently considered what I had just heard, Janice walked in. I got her up to speed on the situation.

"We have not discussed this as a family," Janice told the nurse. "Until that happens the answer you have today is NO. There will be no morphine drip and no removal of her feeding tube."

Several times that day I become aware of Dr. Robinson, who still practices at Municipal, roaming up and down the hallway in front of Mom's room. His presence is an evil specter, a harbinger of things to come. He seems anxious and worried, his head down, his step quick. His furtive glances into my mother's room are disarming. Is he worried about my mother? I think not. He is worried that he soon will be facing a malpractice suit of major proportions and is concerned for the most important person in his life—himself. I mention his passing up and down the hallway to Janice.

She turns without saying a word and closes the curtain so that no one can peer in from the hallway.

The next day Janice was at the hospital early. I arrived a little later. When I came into Mom's room, she was sleeping. Janice was gone, maybe to grab a cup of coffee. I sat next to my mother's bed and began to speak with her.

"Mom, I am so sorry that you have had to endure this sixteen-month struggle. I wish I could have changed that. I really do. Mom ...I want you to know that I am the person I am because of you. The sacrifices you made all those years when we were growing up have made me a loving parent, a supportive and caring grandmother, and a faithful wife. You will always be my mother. I will never forget you. Never. I took her hand gently and held it in mine. She never moved or opened her eyes.

"I want you to know, Mom that I will look after Wanda. I will keep my promises. Mom ... I know that you will let us know what you want us to do. I ask with all the love in my heart ...Mom— ...have ...have you had ...enough?"

She never stirred or opened her eyes to look at me, but I felt the slightest tightening of her hand in mine. I knew what she wanted. As you know when you look into the face of your newborn, I knew that she had given me her answer. She had finally, irrevocably—had enough.

She didn't want to be taken out by a nursing staff anxious to remove her feeding tube, or to be soothed into oblivion with mind-altering drugs. She wanted to do what the old saints of the Bible did. She was ready to give up the ghost of her own free will.

In that moment, I knew that everything that had gone before was right. All the hardship, all the waiting, all the suffering. It had all been in God's timing.

I realized, in that moment, that Mom had known from the beginning. It had taken me sixteen months to understand what she had always understood——it was going to end when she was ready. She never wanted to burden us with making that end-of-life decision. The decision was hers to make ...and hers alone.

Janice came in an hour later. I never shared that moment with her. I felt that as the oldest, Mom was letting me know that she was prepared to cast off the surly bonds of earth, but she was going to do it on her terms. She would not allow anyone else to make that decision for her.   It was hers and hers alone to bear.

I knew before I left that night that she would pass the following day.

Journal Entry:

January 10, 2002

I got a phone call from Janice. "Are you on your way, Jo?"

"Yes, I'm almost to the hospital," I replied.

"Mom's kidneys are failing."

Once all three of us are in the room, we sit in silent vigil. Waiting. Janice and Wanda talk to Mom and tell her how much she is loved.

My emotions today, like so many other days, are all over the place. The one thing I know for sure   is that her battles and her suffering   are nearly over. No more pain, no more depression, no more fatigue that seeps down into the bones.

Soon she will be free of her sickbed. I am sad to have to say goodbye, but know it is what she wants.

"It's time to call the family and let everyone know," I say. We call Patti in Pennsylvania and Lana in California. I hold the phone against Mom's ear so they can tell her goodbye, one last time.

The grandchildren, spouses and friends come to say their goodbyes. My last call is to Father Bill, her favorite priest. As the word goes out to family and close friends, people begin to trickle into the room. It is a tearful but joyful time.

Father Bill arrives at 7:00 pm, he whispers to Mom. He speaks so gently to her. Helping her prepare for the final trip she is about to take.

We gather around her, holding hands. Then together, as we have done every night since our vigil began some sixteen months before, we say the prayer of St. Jude:

Most Holy apostle St Jude. Faithful serv ant and friend of Jesus ....

She gently stops breathing at 7:30 pm. Her eyes never opened. Her last act became her final sacrifice as our beloved mother. The decision to let go was hers. As it should be.

"Blessed is he who perseveres under tial, because when he has stood the test, he will receive the crown of life that God has promise to those who love him."

James 1:12 NV

CHAPTER TWENTY

Lessons Learned

As I reflect on my mother's passing, several questions come to mind. What would I have done differently? What did I learn from the experience? What helped me most along the way?

When anyone goes through a life-changing event, asking questions is one way of ferreting out the truths you have garnered but never fully recognized. The questions and answers listed below are my attempt to come away with the value of the experience and to take those hard fought lessons and turn them into wisdom shared with others.

What would I do differently today faced with the same dilemma? I would ask more questions of everyone, which includes doctors, nurses, adminis-trators and the anesthesiologist—everyone. I would carefully listen to the answers. Educating myself regarding the procedures would be a top priority allowing me to ask informed questions. As Tony Robbins, the great life coach once said, "Want a better life? Ask a better question."

I would also trust my instincts. When faced with a rude, arrogant, and unsympathetic doctor, I would listen to my gut and act on that infor-mation. Hiring a doctor I don't like would be out of the question. There is a reason you don't like that person.

What did I learn from the experience? "Trust but verify. " It is an old Russian proverb. Don't think that because someone wears a medical tag around his or her neck that he or she knows what is best for you and your family.

Most medical professionals are competent and capable, but they are often overwhelmed and car-ing for many patients. In my case, the doctor was not professional and didn't know how best to deal with mother's stenosis. We found that out too late. Had we asked more questions, followed our instincts, and been as informed as possible we may have avoided this outcome.

Examine the facts. Don't hesitate to get a second opinion, know the doctor you are dealing with. Ask the doctor how many procedures like the one he or she will be performing on your loved one he or she has done. Don't be afraid to ask what kind of experience they have with any specialized equipment they plan on using. If you have doubts about the diagnosis or treatment, it never hurts to get a second opinion.

How could I have taken better care of myself during those 500 days? I was conscientious about my physical needs during the 500 days. I ate properly, got a good amount of sleep and exercised.

Physically I was doing well. I didn't realize it at the time, but I was stuffing my emotions. I never spoke to a therapist during or after mother's passing. Writing this book has helped me to work through some of the grief and anxiety that followed. A therapist during the process and after would have been a great release and I am sure would have facilitated healing.

What single thing helped overcome my grief?
My faith in God was always my support. After her
passing, there was peace in knowing she was no
longer in pain. I believe she is looking down on us
now, and saying prayers in heaven for all of us. She
was then and isnow in God's hands.

In the end, my mother decided how she would
pass. That was her parting gift to all of us. I believe that everything   happens for a reason. We
may not know that reason right away. We may
never know the reason.

**What advice would I give to a caregiver in a
similar situation?**   Always follow your heart and
listen to that inner voice. Stay close to your loved
one. Y our suppor t means everything to them in
their time of need.

Stay positive, take breaks from caregiving and
get some sunshine. Go out and have dinner with a
friend, then come back refreshed. Don't feel guilty
about taking some time to unwind, be by yourself
or with a friend. In the end, you are only as good a
caregiver to another as you are to yourself.

Having a strong faith in God has sustained me for most of my life. An abiding faith is a welcome support in a weary world.

Read and research so that you are not accepting the doctor's advice in blind faith, but in knowledge.

Never be afraid to ask questions. Knowledge is power in these situations. Make sure you understand the proposed treatment and never be afraid to ask a question.

Look for support groups in your area. Seek out the support of other caregivers who have or are experiencing what you are going through. If possible, talk to a therapist as you navigate the turbulent waters of long-term caregiving and grief.

Keep the faith and lean on a mighty and understanding God.

EPILOGUE

Twenty years have passed since I sat in that hospital room with Mom. I still see her bright red hair, her painted fingernails and her smiling eyes.

In the midst of tragedy, small blessings can be overlooked. With the passage of time, I realize the many gifts Mom gave me during those *500 Days*. Courage, determination, faith, abiding love of family, and forgiveness.

In the process of writing this   book, I have real- ized what a wise and courageous woman my moth- er t ruly was. More than that, I realize how much wisdom she shared with me. Even in those last 500 days, she gave me the gift of closure.

I think she knew that in order for me to process what happened to her and to "make the best of it" as she always used to say, she knew I would have to write the story. Just as I did when I was a child.

At last, the story is told. The wealth of new friends, new experiences and new opportunities that the book has brought into my life is also a gift from my mother. She knew me well.

As I finish this book, I feel for the first time that I can close that painful, yet beautiful chapter of my life. My mother lived 500 days with pain and suffering, but I wouldn't give back any one of them. During those harrowing 500 days she taught me how to be courageous, how to live my life to the fullest, how to face any dilemma, and the determination to work out a problem by working through it.

The Lawsuit

There was a lawsuit and my sisters and I settled out of court. We were all exhausted and needed to have closure on all the negative things that had happened.

Municipal fired Dr. Robinson. Sadly, after doing a little research on the Internet, I saw that he is still "practicing medicine" in a small town in California.

I hope that by sharing my experiences, both my mistakes and the things I did right, it will help another person who may be going through a similar situation.

Nowadays I stay busy working on seminars and going to book signings, but Mom is with me. I know she looks down and says to herself, "Good girl. Great job."

Then I'm sure she breaks into a yodel!

"

Where there is love, there is the possibility of pain.

Where there is pain, there is the possibility of suffering.

Where there is suffering, there is the possibility of a savior.

Where there is a savior, there is the possibility of redemption.

Where there is redemption, there is the possibility of restoration.

—Ravi Zacharias

ACKNOWLEDGMENT

I want to thank those who helped me turn this book from a dream into a reality. Thank you Aunt Patti Whisler for painstakingly compil ing our family history, including some of Mom's story. That history helped me to believe that I could get this done.

Janice, thank you for the diaries, which chronicled every procedure and medical event during Mom's sixteen-month hospital ization. The diaries were invaluable in establishing a timeline and to capture the day-to-day challenges ofMom's story.

I thank my sister Wanda who never wavered in her support.

I want to thank my son, Jeremy, who was strong for all of us during those long hospital days. I am grateful to his two girls, Miranda and Julia, my beautiful granddaughters— thank you all for being there. Miranda, thank you for your work on the website and social media. Thank you Julia for providing me moral support in those early days.

Jimmy, thank you for standing by me without complaint while I traveled away from home for weeks at a time in support of my mother. You gave me peace for those short hours I was home during her hospitalization. I am grateful for your on-going support of this book project.

I want to thank my nephew, Jason, for his diligence in visiting Mom during his rare leaves from his duties in the Air Force.

All of you contributed to helping me tell Mom's story. Without each of you, it might never have been completed.

I know Mom is proud that we, as a family, have come together to see it through and tell her story.

ABOUT JO ANN WILLS

For as long as I can remember, I have yearn ed to be an entre-preneur. This book is my first real foray into the world of en-trepreneurship. It seems I have been working my whole life   for someone else's dream From   selling lemonade on the front sidewalk at seven to   helping my dad at the dog pound at twelve, I was always working.

In my adolescence, I helped my mother stick labels onto envelopes for bulk mailings when she worked at American Advertising Company.

After high school, I took a job instead of attending college to help Mom support the household.

As an adult, I was a dental assistant for twenty years. Later I became a teaching assistant for special needs kids. I worked with the kids for twenty-two years.

The one thing I never saw myself doing was writing a book. However, I made a promise to my mother to tell her story and in the process tell my own. At last, I have kept that promise. Thank you Mom for all you did for my sisters and me and thank you for teaching us all how to be courageous and stalwart in the face of immense challenges.

Because of your example, I was able to persevere and write your story. My wish is that my story can help you or someone you love who may be going through a similar situation.

Stay Connected with Jo Ann

To stay connected with Jo Ann and learn more about caregiving and patient advocacy, visit www.JoAnnWillsAuthor.com. You can email her at JoAnnWillsAuthor@gmail.com. To have Ms. Wills speak to your school, group, organization or association, contact her by email.

Thank you for reading this book. If you liked the book, please take a moment to write a review or to send me your thoughts.

Jo Ann Wills

Helpful Websites for Caregivers

www.healthadvocateresources.com

www.allianceforpatientaccess.org

www.patientsource.com

www.panfoundation.org

Helpful Websites & Associations

www.GildasHouse.com

www.betterhelp.com

www.onwardhealthcare.com

Recommended Reading for Caregivers

Hospital Stay Handbook; Jari Holland Buck

Right Care, Right Now; Stuart D. Heaslet

Stand in the Way; Betty Tomsing

Malpractice; Dr. Larry Schlachter

Trust Your Doctor but Not That Much: Be Your Own Best Health Care Advocate, Regina S. Wedner

My Medical Journal; Route 19 Publishing

Patients' Needs Advocates, Gilda Tuttlebee

Patient Advocate Handbook: How to Find and Use Your Voice in Healthcare; Liz Crocker and Clare Crocker

Quench Your Burning Mouth and Tongue; Dr. Arcoma Gonzales Lambert

Made in the USA
Columbia, SC
02 November 2021